First published in England 1986 by
Leader Books Limited,
Barford Court,
Lampard Lane,
Churt,
Surrrey.

ISBN 0 950 96981 X

Printed in England by Arrowhead Printing Limited,
Unit 3, Park Works, Kingsley, Bordon, Hampshire.

A TALENT FOR LIVING

THE LIFE AND ART OF
TWELVE REMARKABLE ARTISTS

BY
MARC ALEXANDER

Photographs taken specially for this book were by
the author and Simon Alexander

LEADER BOOKS

CONTENTS

50
Derrick Vandek

58
Charles Fowler

66
Paul Driver

76
Margeret Greig

86
Albert Baker

96
Joy Clarke

108
Kris Kirk

120
Heather Strudwick

FOREWORD

So many stories in this book convey the struggle I have seen in countless disabled people's lives. The struggle, not only against disability but the struggle to achieve against great odds.

Marc Alexander provides us with a simple, matter of fact, often detailed account of the lives of 12 severely disabled people, all totally different but each revealing the talent and ability to paint with either their mouth or their foot.

To be shown how they achieve this is to understand something of the joy and fulfilment that, against all the odds, they bring not only to themselves but to all those who see their paintings.

The success stories of all the people in this book can probably be summed up by one moment in Heather Strudwick's life. This was the day when she was made a full salaried member of the Mouth and Foot Painter's Association, and was able to write to the Social Security office to inform them, that after receiving assistance for over twenty years, she was now able to support herself.

This is a stimulating book and I warmly recommend it.

Leonard Cheshire

INTRODUCTION: SARAH BIFFIN

Sarah Biffen was the first recorded British mouth painter. Born without arms or legs in Somerset, she lived from 1784 to 1850 and during her adult life she managed to make a living by demonstrating her ability to paint with a brush held between her teeth in a travelling side-show. Although her attraction to the fairground public was as a novelty — freak shows were very popular in those days — Sarah in fact was a very talented artist and actually had a painting accepted by the Royal Academy. Her technical skill increased to a point where she could not only paint excellent miniatures but do embroidery using her teeth to guide the needle.

In these more benevolent times disabled artists do not have to appear alongside the bearded lady and the tattooed man to survive, but this makes the effort put into acquiring their skill no less remarkable. Today it would be unthinkable for disabled people to be left to their own devices, to get by or starve; through state and health authorities society does look after the disabled in a way which could not be imagined in Sarah Biffen's day. But for some disabled people the Welfare State is not enough. No matter what their physical problems are, they long for the one thing that is the most difficult to achieve — to support themselves financially and thus to be able to live outside institutions and enjoy the everyday independence that the able-bodied take for granted.

This book tells the stories of a dozen disabled people who, through their ability to paint, have achieved this goal.

That they have been able to do this is thanks to the vision of Erich Stegmann who lost the use of his hands and arms at the age of three. Later he became so adept at mouth painting that he succeeded in his dream of becoming a professional artist; his attention then turned to others with similar problems around the world. Erich Stegmann believed that they could do as he had done if given the chance, and in order to give them that chance he founded the international Association of Mouth and Foot Painting Artists.

The aim of the organisation is twofold, to assist disabled people with potential painting talent to improve the standard of their work through assistance with tuition and special equipment, and to market the work of its members so that they can carry on freed from financial worry. When a person who has been given a student scholarship can produce work which is judged by an independent panel of experts as being equal to the standard of able-bodied artists who sell their work professionally, he or she becomes a full member of the Association.

Members' work is used for Christmas and birthday cards, calendars and notelets, and it is from the sale of these products that the Association receives the income which is redistributed in monthly payments to the artists who usually recieve an annual bonus as well. Another activity is the organization of exhibitions of the members' work and the proceeds from each picture sold goes directly to the artist who painted it. The Association also has a trust fund for the training of handicapped children in arts and crafts.

To my mind the best aspect of the scheme is that once a disabled artist is accepted as a member of the Association his or her monthly payments are guaranteed for life. This means that if through increasing disability an artist is faced with the prospect of not being able to continue painting, the haunting fear of financial disaster and the loss of independence is avoided.

It should be remembered that the Association of Mouth and Foot Painting Artists is not a charity and therefore does not qualify for any charitable assistance. It is, in effect, a worldwide business partnership between artists who are proud of the commercial ability to support themselves, and whose very last wish is to be on the receiving end of charity.

In the writing of this book I found one of its most interesting aspects was the diversity of the artists I visited. They come from widely differing backgrounds, are of different ages and their disabilities obviously vary, ranging from the results of accidents to nerve-affecting diseases such as poliomyelitis. What I fould cruelly ironic was that some were especially active physically before they were stricken, for example Kris Kirk was an amazing young sportsman and athlete, Derrick Vandek was one of the foremost balancing acts in the country and Elizabeth Twistington Higgins was a professional ballet dancer and teacher.

Another thing that several of the artists have in common is the helpful effect that pre-disability experience has given them. One of the difficulties for an artist without the use of hands is in studying the object to be painted. A vase of flowers can be placed before you as a subject for a still life picture, but it is frustratingly impossible to alter the arrangement yourself or handle a flower to observe its formation and colouring.

This is when specialized knowledge acquired when the artist was able-bodied comes into its own. Margaret Greig loved nothing better than riding before she contracted polio, now a lot of her best work features horses; ex-RAF pilot Peter Spencer is in his element painting aircraft on canvas; Joy Clarke once worked in horticulture and this gives added realism to her flower studies, while Elizabeth Twistington Higgins' dancers are now world famous.

In meeting these artists, one thing which came across to me in every case was the genuine love of painting they felt, and the fact that while they were engaged in it they were not disabled — art has given them a new dimension in which their imaginations are freed from wheelchairs and medical appliances. It would be wrong to think of them as clever disabled people who have learned to paint, they are artists who have discovered their own talents depite disability.

Understandably their handicaps have affected their work as far as progress in developing the necessary skills is concerned. A mouth painting artist who has the use of his legs and can walk round his studio will obviously find painting easier than someone who is totally paralysed, while some artists have to contend with breathing problems on top of everything else.

This is one of the reasons why an artist cannot be judged by the length of time spent as a student before being admitted to full membership of the Association. Each individual has had different difficulties to surmount, but all agree that what matters is the end result on canvas. Paul Driver said to me, 'When some journalists interview us all they want is a sob story. They are only interested in one's private life and do not understand that the most important thing is what one produces as an artist.'

This book was not planned merely to be a collection of biographies but also as an 'art book' demonstrating the work of artists who happen to have acquired their skills through years and years of battling against almost impossible odds. Of such work Albert Schweitzer once said, 'The pictures give you an idea of the artistic capability of the people who painted them, but something else is shown — courage to live. This is a spiritual gift which we have to accept from these artists and may we be thankful for it.'

The old Russian artist monks who painted icons used to mix their paints with holy water in order to enhance the spiritual value of their work — here you will see work of artists whose brushes have been figuratively dipped in blood and sweat and the occasional tear.

Marc Alexander

Liverpool Daily Post
WEDNESDAY OCTOBER 2, 1940.

Sarah Biffen

Ninety years ago to-day there died in Liverpool one of the most extraordinary characters the town has ever had, Sarah Biffen, of 8 Duke Street. Originally a Somerset girl, she was born in 1784 without arms or hands. Yet, with her mouth and the aid of an attachment to her shoulder, she rose to national fame as a miniature-painter of exquisite delicacy, and is twice mentioned in the works of Dickens.

The Royal Society of Arts conferred a medal on her, and she was kindly received by the Royal Family. In her declining years she was granted a Civil List pension, and Richard Rathbone organised a public subscription for her. The Hornby Library here contains several valuable examples of her art, including a portrait of Hugh F. Hornby (the founder) as a young man. The artist's grave is in St. James's Gardens, below the Cathedral.

* * *

'Disabled artists of the world, unite!'

ARNULF ERICH STEGMANN

DRESSED in an old, very comfortable and very paint-stained coat, the artist hunched before his easel, engrossed in the street scene which, with confident strokes, he was transferring to his canvas. As always when a painter is working out of doors passers by paused to watch, only on this occasion it was not to compare the half-finished picture with the original but to stare at the painter himself.

'Poor man,' someone uttered. 'He's crippled . . .'

'Look mummy, he's holding the brush in his mouth . . .'

'We must give him something . . .'

A coin dropped into the artist's hat which he had thoughtlessly placed beside his folding stool. More coins tinkled after it, then a pound note fluttered from the hand of a generous tourist, and several dollars followed the fall of sterling.

Suddenly aware of what was happening, the artist leaned his massive blond head forwards and released the paint brush holder from between his teeth. The mood was ruined — he was once again reminded that he was an object of curiousity not because of what he was painting but because his arms were paralysed.

The money in the hat was well-intended — Arnulf Erich Stegmann was aware of that — but what he was never able to accept was pity.

'Pity's the worst thing I have had to fight all my life,' he declared. 'I do not want pity. Most people are so extremely considerate, they believe I am dependent on their help. That drives me mad.'

Yet, in his old clothes and with his useless hands thrust into his pockets as he painted, what else could he expect unless he locked himself away in his studio?

'I could not blame the givers for their action,' he explained later. 'What they saw was a man in a wrinkled, paint-bespattered coat who sat in the street and painted pictures with his mouth! Why, if one gave a coin to a street acrobat, should one not give one to a man performing such an artistic feat!

'I had to figure a way out of the dilemma. Either I had to give up painting out of doors altogether, which I did not want to do, or else I must show by my appearance that I was not dependent on pity or alms. How could they know that my pictures brought me in more than they had in their pockets? So when I worked out of doors I dressed myself in good shirts, expensive ties, and my newest suits.'

His plan worked. Onlookers no longer regarded him as some unfortunate seeking street charity through his remarkable ability — remarkable in that he could daub paint on canvas at all! — but as a successful painter.

From then on no more coins fell into his hat, and to his pleasure more notice was taken of his skill with his brush than the technique he was forced to employ.

This was always the foremost tenet in Erich Stegmann's philosophy, which he once summed up when he told the German author J.H. Roesler, 'I want my pictures to sell because they are good. What difference does it make how a picture is painted? A painter paints from his heart what his eyes see. The picture then wants to find friends. Pictures are like children who leave home. Nobody asks them whether their father has lost a foot or an arm. Why then should it arise about my pictures?'

Credo!

When Erich Stegmann was born in Darmstadt in 1912 his bank clerk father — in common with the other citizens of Germany and indeed Europe — could have had little idea of the vast catastrophe which lay ahead. There was a sense of prosperity and security in the air reflecting the fruits of the industrial revolution and the new middle and professional classes it had engendered. Along with a material prosperity enjoyed by all members of society, new and daring ideas were abroad. In that year names in the news were Picasso, Bonnard, Marc Chagall, Ravel, Debussy, Utrillo. In France Henri Alain-Fournier, so soon to die in battle at St Remy, published *Le Grand Meaulnes*; in Germany the Socialists were declaring their anti-war commitment and calling for international solidarity of the working people.

This comfortable yet exciting world was to change forever when little Erich was two years old ... the assassin's shots at Sarajevo signalled the conflict which for the first time in history was to be known as a 'world' war.

The war was still in its early stages and still a cause for patriotic enthusiasm on all sides, when a family crisis overtook the Stegmanns — Erich became ill and the doctor pronounced that he was suffering from polio. When the initial attack subsided, and Erich's parents were reassured that their son's life would be spared, it was found that he had been left with paralysed hands and arms while his legs had been affected to a lesser degree.

Over six decades on Erich still recalled how his earliest memories were those of frustration because he could not do things like his brother and sister.

Of these the most vivid went back to when he was five years old and, like his brother and sister, he had to accept the family form of punishment for some childish misdemeanour. Frau Stegmann did not believe in smacking her children when she felt that some particular piece of naughtiness deserved parental response, her method was simple and far more effective — the culprit was undressed and sent to bed for a period of time related to the heinousness of the act he or she had committed.

As it was the policy of Erich's parents to treat him as much like his brother and sister as possible, he was not immune to being whisked off to bed. Sometimes the children's mother would forget when the sentence was over. When this happened Erich's brother and sister, who had been watching the clock, merely jumped out of bed, pulled on their clothes and resumed their play. Not so Erich. With his useless arms straight by his side, he had to remain prone until his mother finally remembered his plight or was finally summoned to the bedroom by his cries of outrage.

This sense of outrage suffered by the little boy was to prove his most valuable asset. By the time he started school he had decided that if he was to lead a satisfactory life — a life in which figuratively he could not have to bellow for his freedom — he must earn a great deal of money. Love of money might be the root of all evil, but Erich saw it as the key to enjoying the things that his healthy companions expected as their right — travel, a base to live and work, independence and, above all, freedom from pity.

As he stood in the playground of his first school, watching his fellows running about with waving arms in the exuberance of playtime, he must have wondered how someone like him who always had to remain in the corner, someone condemned always to watch sport from the sideline, could ever compete. Each morning in the classroom he found it an ordeal to look on while the others took their pencils and began their writing exercises while he sat stiff-armed at his desk, a pathetic figure who still had to be dressed by his mother.

There was only one thing he could do, and he did it.

He clamped a pencil between his teeth and laboriously tried to copy the letters and sentences from the blackboard.

His first efforts made him want to weep but the tears were held back. It was enough to be seen as a cripple, but never as a weeping cripple. Besides, he would not be able to wipe away those embarrassing tears. Instead he held the pencil until he almost bit it through, and to the fascinated interest of the class continued trying to make his letters. How much better he found it when he held a paint brush between his teeth. There was something so delightful about the way the paint lines followed the brush, something sensuous about the way the primary colours appeared to glow on the paper in front of him.

Every time painting lessons came round Erich Stegmann became more and more convinced that art held the answer to his problems. He would become a professional artist and make a great deal of money! But how hard it was to make those tantalizing colours obey him. So often his efforts resembled the work of the modern art movement which attracted so much attention after the war, only Erich Stegmann had not intended his work to appear like that!

He remained at his easel while his schoolfellows were at play, urged on by the need to prove that not only was he as good as they, but that he could do better. These efforts were not unnoticed by his teachers who began to realize his potential. They forgot that the boy clamped a brush beteen his teeth when it became obvious that his work was not clever compensation for a handicap but that he had an inherent artistic ability. The result was that in 1927 Erich was admitted to the Oz School of Art, a great honour for any young student, and this drove him to greater efforts.

'I was allowed to do live models at the age of sixteen, a privilege seldom granted to students of that age,' he later recalled. 'I worked like mad for I felt I had to make a success of it. I was one of the best in my class in portrait painting, and won a scholarship from the Lord Mayor of Nuremberg, where my parents had gone to live, to work for one year in the studio of a famous artist. The choice was left to me. I went to von Kormendy, a Hungarian.'

At the age of twenty-two, Erich Stegmann felt confident enough to leave home and share a studio with his brother-in-law.

At last life seemed to smile on the young artist; he had won his independence, he was painting professionally and now there was his girlfriend Bobby Hartmann. The only cloud on the young man's horizon was one that he shared with many young intellectuals — the increasing power of the Nationalist Socialist movement. The year before Erich Stegmann left his parents' home Hitler had been appointed Chancellor of Germany; the German Catholic and Social Democrat Parties were suppressed, Communists were blamed for the Reichstag fire, and the first concentration camps were established.

With his obsession about personal independence colouring his political outlook, the student Erich Stegmann had never withheld his views on the Nazis and actively opposed them. This resulted in his arrest as 'an enemy of the Nazi State' just before Christmas, 1934, and for the next fifteen months he was held in gaol. Here his demands for drawing materials were turned down and, carrying the extra burden of bodily disability, his health suffered terribly. Finally the medical officer at the local prison decided that he should be transferred to the Munich prison at Ettstrasse because his physical state had deteriorated so badly, though this did not prevent him being threatened with execution when his behaviour annoyed his escorts.

It was here — on March 4, his birthday — that he was informed that the case against him had been dropped by the police through lack of evidence. Later, as a result of his experience, he was made an honorary member of the board of directors of the *Vereinigung der Verfolgten des Nazi regimes* — the Association of Persecutees by the Nazi Government.

Two months after he was released Erich Stegmann married Bobby Hartmann, and returned to painting and running the publishing house he had established in 1932. Throughout the rest of the thirties and the early forties, his opposition to the Nazis continued and in 1944 he found it necessary to go into hiding, staying at St Jodoch near Brenner, in Hagnau on Lake Constance and on Our Lady Island in Lake Chiemsee where the respective mayors shared his anti-Nazi sentiments.

Two children were born to Erich and Bobby but by the end of the war he and Bobby had parted. Some time afterwards he married his second wife, Traudi Billmeir, with whom he had two more children. Later it took all of Erich Stegmann's strength of will to face up to their tragic deaths when they were killed in road accidents five years apart. Yet, however life treated him, he continued to paint and in the late 1950s began to hold one-man exhibitions in such cities at Athens, Rome and Jerusalem, to name but three of the many.

It became one of his main delights to visit the island of Burano in the Venetian lagoon, and was well known to tourists for its lace as Murano is for its glass. Here he loved to paint the shabby harbour and the distinctive old houses dreaming about the water. He had started going there soon after the war and fell in love with the place to the extent of buying a plot of land running down to the sea, and parking a green caravan on it to which he returned each summer.

Erich Stegmann's Burano oil paintings are very distinctive with their rich and sombre colours which, as those who have visited the island will agree, accurately reflect the sense of place. The walls of the houses are dark reds and browns, with distinctive greenish-white window and door frames, which are mirrored in the still water along the black hulls of Venetian boats.

While the heavy positive oils were very much Erich Stegmann's style — reflecting the strength and aggression of his personality — they were not his only style. His water colours had a much lighter touch, especially his portraits, but these too were only part of his artistic repertoire. It seems as though he had decided to master as many techniques as possible, which included using the crayon-on-stone technique for litho pictures and, with the handles of the tools held in his mouth, the carving out of lino and wood cuts. Nothing deterred him when it came to artistic expression, even to the painting of life size figures on the wall of a house, which is a traditional art form in southern Germany. Perhaps the most spectacular of all, from a technical point of view, were his wood carvings which seem almost an impossibility when one remembers that the chisels had to be gripped by his teeth.

One of the hardest technical challenges he had to face was when he was still at art school where he had to copy recognised masterpieces such as the Mona Lisa. The originals were finely detailed, full of subtle colour tones such as the effect of light on fabric, yet he managed to reproduce with his mouth-held brush the famous works which had been accomplished by the hands of classical painters. The art historian Richard Hiepe wrote: 'The compulsory examination pieces, such as copying Old Masters, Arnulf Erich Stegmann did as sensitively and precisely as any other. His copies of Brueghel, and Cranach's "Venus and Amor" today still hang in his home at Deisenhofen near Munich. They could not be improved upon . . ."

Soon after the Second World War had ended and Erich Stegmann was able to consider normal life again, he found himself giving a lot of thought to those around the world who must be in a similar predicament, people with artistic ability but who, as a result of physical disability, were only able to express it through brushes held in their mouths or between their toes. Many, he guessed, were probably much more handicapped than himself — he, at least, could walk about — but there must be paraplegic artists condemned to spend their lives in bed or in wheelchairs. No doubt there were those whose talent could be developed if only they could receive special training. How did they manage? he wondered.

Because of his aggressive determination, coupled with his artistic ability, he had fulfilled his boyhood promise to himself to earn enough money to pay for his independence, but how about the others? And what was being done to get their work before the public so that they could be respected rather than pitied?

In his travels he had always sought out disabled artists, and as a result a bold plan formed in his mind which could easily have had the slogan 'Disabled artists of the world, unite!'

In 1956 he formed the Association of Mouth and Foot Painting Artists which, because of its international nature, had its headquarters in Vaduz, Liechtenstein. Twenty-five years after the association was formed a convention of its members was held in Madrid attended by members from thirty-six countries. In the preface to the publication marking this anniversary the aims of the Association were set out thus: 'There are artists living in various countries of the world who paint with their mouth or foot. Their disability makes it particularly difficult for them to establish the necessary contacts which would enable them to obtain commercial benefit from their work. The Association now gives them a foundation on which to base their livelihood, and to allow them to devote themselves to their art, free from hardship and worry. To achieve this objective, the Association endeavours firstly to trace all mouth and foot painting artists as far as possible, induce them to join, and secondly, to approach suitable publishers to request them to publish the work of the mouth and foot painting artists. In addition, the Association encourages developing mouth and foot artists by granting stipends.

To become a full member of the Association the artist must satisfy an independent board that his or her work compares favourably with that of non-disabled professional artists. When this procedure has been satisfactorily completed the artist is put on a regular monthly salary which will guarantee independence for life. This is regardless of output, and in effect means that should an artist's disability increase so that painting is no longer possible, the income will still continue ensuring that freedom from financial anxiety will be maintained.

After 1956 Erich Stegmann, as President and Founder of the Association, travelled the world many times to promote the work of its members by exhibition and to organise the training of disabled people whose latent talent suggested that it would be possible for them to reach an artistic competence which would qualify them for full membership.

During those years Erich Stegmann received many honours in different countries, including the Officier de l'ordre du merite, Paris, Kinstpreis 1974 des Vdk Deutschlands and the University Citation of the State University of New York for outstanding humanitarian service.

It is a long time since the child Erich Stegmann first held a bush between his teeth, but the determination it represented in those far off days achieved much more than an ability to paint his own pictures professionally. When he died in 1984 scores of disabled artists were able to lead independent lives thanks to his inspiration, while today the Association which he created continues to help more such painters to realize their creative ambitions.

'I'll Never Climb Everest, But . . .'

BRUCE PEARDON

'I felt pretty devastated for the first fifteen minutes when I was told that I would not get the use of my limbs back,' says Bruce Peardon in his typical matter-of-fact way. 'But after that I just concentrated on getting on with life. I was lucky that I was young, and young people are adaptable . . .'

And get on with life he did, so that today he is regarded not only as a commercial artist but also as one of Australia's serious painters. The fact that his work is done with a mouth-held brush makes no difference to the public, who visit his exhibitions and buy his work, or to him.

'To paint with a brush held between my teeth — apart from when I bit the end off — seems to be a perfectly natural way to paint,' he explains. 'And I found it so from the start. We are all part of the animal kingdom on this planet, and animals have a knack of adapting very quickly to changes in their condition — if a dog loses a leg you'll soon see it running around just as well on three. It was the same for me. When I could no longer use my hands I found I could write almost immediately with a pencil held between my teeth. When I came to painting I had no difficulty in using a brush in this way — what I really had to work hard at was learning the correct technique of painting.'

Bruce Peardon was born near Brisbane in 1945, the fourth in a family of six children which was equally divided into girls and boys. At the age of fifteen he joined the navy as a junior recruit, doing a year's training in Perth, Western Australia, after which he was transferred to Flinders Naval Depot in Victoria.

On 14 October, 1962, he went on leave with a friend and it was on the return journey that his accident happened.

'It was a long way back to base,' he says. 'I had been driving back through the night until I was pretty bushed, so I curled up on the back seat to get some sleep while my friend took the wheel — and then next thing I knew was opening my eyes in hospital. My friend had dozed off, the car left the road and my spine was injured in the crash.

'It wasn't too bad for the first three weeks, then I had a relapse and after that I had to face the fact that I was paralysed.'

In the Austin Hospital, in Melbourne, Bruce was fascinated to see two fellow patients painting by means of brushes held in their mouths. They were Bill Mooney and the late James Meath, and they explained that they were members of the Association of Mouth and Foot Painting Artists.

'The fact that they painted with their mouths inspired me to do the same,' Bruce says. 'I had been a hobby artist and I think I had a fairly natural talent for drawing and painting. I did not find any difficulty with the technique of using the brush — what I really had to study was the basics of how to paint properly, perspective and colour values and so on. One curious thing was that being left-handed I found that I always held the brush in the left corner of my mouth. By 1964 I had reached a stage that I was accepted as a student by the Mouth and Foot Painting Artists.'

Not long after this Bruce was involved, with some fellow disabled patients in the hospital where circumstances had forced him to remain, in what was then a unique pioneering project. Wishing to prove to the government that it could be cheaper for the disabled to live outside hospital, the group acquired a house and set up what could be described as a wheelchair commune. Today such schemes are not uncommon in Australia, but twenty years

Bruce Peardon seen here with his son Ben

ago it was a break-through for the disabled, though finally those involved had to give up the project through lack of finance.

Bruce had no wish to return to hospital and, helped by his income from the Association, he was able to get a house of his own in which a young married couple looked after him in return for accommodation. Meanwhile he continued to work at improving his painting. Because of practical difficulties in attending art school, he continued to teach himself.

'I learned the most by studying the works of the Old Masters in art books, and by going to galleries,' he says. 'In 1970, after I had been a student for six years, I became a full member of the Association, and apart from the work I did for it I had several one-man exhibitions, and while I shall never aspire to the master category, I had my small successes with these shows.

'I think that there is too much pretentiousness in the art world — people think that one has to be a Van Gogh, or starve to death in a garret. I believe that one has to paint to live, and therefore I look upon myself as a commercial painter in that if I am commissioned to do a landscape, or a portrait, that is exactly what I have to do.

'Of course, I do enjoy painting for myself, and these are the pictures we have in our home. When I am painting for my own pleasure I cover a number of subjects; I particulary like to paint seascapes, "old world" still life, and character studies which show people in situations whereby the picture tells a story. I am also very keen on Australian landscapes and a country such as ours offers the artist a great variety ranging from tropical rain forest to the desert environment.'

Bruce's work for the Association of Mouth and Foot Painting Artists, which is reproduced on cards and calendars, usually depicts children in various situations. These pictures have an air of gentle humour about them and prove to be very popular with the public. For these studies Bruce paints in gouache because of its opaque colour effect; for his more serious work he uses oils and less frequently water colours.

A year after Bruce had graduated to full membership of the Association he met, and began going out with, a nurse named Christine Halliday. In 1973 they were married and in 1976 they designed and built their own house in a bushland setting seventeen miles south-west of Brisbane.

'It's surrounded by lovely trees with plenty of animal and bird life — an easy place to live in and very conducive to painting,' Bruce says. 'Being the son of a builder came in very handy when I organized the subcontracting of the building. I had been quite good at trade work and I did find it frustrating not to be able to do any of the physical work myself.'

A son was born to Christine and Bruce in 1983. Christened Benjamin, his proud father describes him as a 'vibrant little fellow who keeps us both young'.

One result of his arrival was that for a while Bruce became more aware and frustrated at being disabled than at any other time in the twenty years he had been a quadriplegic. When Benjamin cried he was unable to cuddle him or pick him up when he fell over. But as Benjamin grew this passed — if he was in trouble he was able to go to his dad, or Bruce would call him to his wheelchair.

'What is remarkable is the way he helps me,' says Bruce. 'In this respect he is years ahead of his actual age. He understands what I need and happily brings things for me, and he even helps me with my hoist apparatus. A pretty good rapport seems to be developing between us.'

Benjamin is now of an age to be fascinated by his father's painting and endeavours to draw himself — by holding a pencil in his mouth!

Bruce finds him an ideal model for his child studies, working from the many photographs that Christine takes of him in order to capture a certain smile or a fleeting expression. Bruce's interest in children spread beyond his canvases when a book he wrote and illustrated was published under the title of *Charley the Chimney-sweep and Sooty.* He is currently working on another book for children with the text in verse based on the animals of Australia. Writing is something which he would like to develop much further, having been encouraged by letters he has received from all over the world in appreciation of *Charley*.

'As well as the children's book, I am working on an adult novel,' he says. 'I use an electric typewriter which has a correcting ribbon, and I cannot think of anything more useful than that when you type with a stick held in your mouth. I wish such machines had been available years ago when I first started to type and made so many mistakes.'

Today Bruce leads a packed life. He and Christine have been twice round the world in order to attend international meetings of Mouth and Foot Artists, and they travel extensively in Australia by car which enables Christine to photograph scenes which Bruce will later put on canvas. One frequent trip which they both enjoy is the twelve-hundred mile journey to Adelaide to visit his parents-in-law. At home when he is not painting he enjoys watching sport — especially cricket and Rugby union — on television and listening to music, his catholic tastes including British and Australian folk songs and classical music, Beethoven being his favourite composer.

Another of his activities which he regards as highly important is visiting schools where he not only demonstrates his method of painting and talks about other disabled artists but addresses the pupils on road and water safety.

'I believe it is important that people such as myself who have been injured in road accidents confront the children with what can happen if due care isn't taken,' he declares.

Like the other artists described in this book Bruce displays no bitterness about being disabled.

'It's not a thing you would choose,' he says with a hint of Aussie humour, 'but Chris and I make the best of it. I know I'll never climb Everest but most of the time I am not aware of being handicapped.'

'Exceptional Services to Humanity'

Peter Spencer and his wife June with children Robin and Jill

PETER SPENCER M.B.E.

THE telegram from the Air Ministry was something which Nelson and Beatrice Spencer — like so many other parents of boys in the RAF — had dreaded receiving. It read: 'We regret to inform you that your son, Flt. Sgt. Peter Nelson Spencer, is critically ill in St Richard's Hospital, Chichester.'

For a moment there was relief — he was still *alive!* He had not been killed on one of his daily flights across the Channel to the battlefields of Europe! But this was followed by sickening questions to which the bald words of the telegram held no clue: What had happened to him? How ill was he to be described as critical? Was he dying, and could they get to him in time?

These thoughts haunted the couple as they left their home in Wallasey, in what is now known as Merseyside, and began a nightmare journey on wartime trains which travelled so slowly that they did not arrive at their destination until the next day.

At St Richard's they were shown into a room where their only son lay in a hospital bed with his face as white as the bandages that swathed his body, bandages which did not hide the fact that his right arm was missing. As she took this in Beatrice collapsed but when she came round again she summoned up enough strength to go back into the room to be beside her boy, waiting for him to open his eyes from his drug-induced coma . . .

Peter Spencer was fifteen years old at the outbreak of the Second World War and a pupil of Oldershaw Grammar School. When the Air Training Corps was formed in Wallasey he joined 273 Squadron and his enthusiasm for it was as keen as it had been for the school sports in which he had delighted. Later he became the first cadet to become a Flight Sergeant.

When he applied to enlist in the RAF the recruiting officer asked him what he wanted to be in the service.

'A night fighter, sir,' he replied.

'Why, can you see in the dark?'

'I've been eating a lot of carrots, sir,' he said, referring to the wartime myth — invented to mislead the enemy about British radar — that the RAF's night-flying pilots lived on a diet of carrots. The recruiting officer roared with laughter, and Peter was in.

Following this he was awarded a short-term scholarship to Pembroke College, to study subjects relating to flying, where he joined the Cambridge University Air Squadron. When this period ended he was sent to a grading school to decide his aptitude for flying. The result was positive and in the summer of 1943 he left Liverpool in an unescorted transport ship *Pasteur* en route for the No 5 British Flying Training School at Clewiston in Florida. After the grey life of wartime Britain with its dangers and shortages, Florida was literally a new world for the young Englishman. Apart from the sunshine and abundance of food there was an exciting social life, it seemed everyone wanted to entertain the cadets who would soon be going into action against Hitler. But a sombre note was struck when they were warned that two cadets had been killed on every course.

'It was an uncomfortable feeling to think that two of us might not make it — that it might be me in a training crash,' says Peter today. 'And sure enough two of our chaps did get killed. Altogether over thirty RAF cadets died during training at Clewiston, and there is a special cemetery for them where there is a ceremony of remembrance held every year.'

Peter was particularly popular. With his dark curly hair, deep set grey eyes and easy smile, he was the embodiment of what Americans thought of as an RAF Pilot. Added to this was his talent at the piano keyboard which he had begun studying at the age of seven. At parties he was always the centre of attraction as he entertained with current hit tunes.

Apart from the bright lights — so very bright after Britain's nightly black-outs — and the off-duty social whirl, for Peter there was the pure joy of flying, a love of which has remained with him throughout his life. He received his 'Wings' in February, 1944, having been rated as an 'above aver-age pilot', and two months later he was back in Wallasey for a brief leave with his parents before joining a training unit to fly Dakotas, the workhorses of Transport Command. Operational flying began in September when he was sent to 512 Squadron of 46 Group Transport Command at Broadwell in Oxfordshire.

From then on he and three crew mates flew their Dakota regularly across the Channel, carrying supplies to army units spearheading the invasion of France. Often they had to land on prefabricated runways made from strips of metal mesh in open fields, and after their cargo had been unloaded it was replaced by wounded soldiers to be ferried back to England. As the young pilot watched them being carried aboard his aircraft — men brought straight from the battle zone, some of whom had lost limbs — he could not imagine what life could hold for him.

Early in February, 1945, Peter was promoted to Flight Sergeant and the next month he and his mates were flying in support of the Rhine crossing from which their aircraft returned pockmarked by flak. On March 27 he had a free day and was sitting at the mess piano when a friend known as Smithy entered and said that he had volunteered for a 'hush-hush' job.

'Anyone want to come along?' he asked cheerfully.

Peter stood up, followed by another friend Ken Thwaites. It turned out that the job was to fly four officers to Rheims in an Anson aircraft, but after they had taken off bad weather forced them to make an unscheduled landing at Ford. Here they had a leisurely lunch and at mid-afternoon a truck arrived to take them back to their plane across the tarmac.

Ken Thwaites looked out of the window when the noise of a taxi-ing air-craft reached them.

'Only a Mosquito,' he reported.

The words were just out of his mouth when the bomber's starboard prop-eller sliced into the truck, amputating Peter's arm. After that his next mem-ory was coming to in hospital. As he realized that he had lost his right arm and that his left was paralysed, the first thought that flashed into his mind was, 'I'll never play the piano again!'

The pain which swept his body seemed too much for a human to bear, and he had to be injected with morphine. Later he surfaced from blissful oblivion to find his mother and father beside his bed, and with a great effort he managed to give them a smile.

When Beatrice and Nelson Spencer left their son's room, the matron warned them to be prepared for the worst.

'In cases like this the patient invariably dies of depression,' she said mat-ter-of-factly. Although Peter was to have bouts of intense depression and the feeling that without his arms he could be of no use to himself or anyone else, he lived to disprove the matron's words. The years passed with him staying in various hospitals and rehabilitation centres during which he was hardly ever free from pain. Like other amputees, he experienced phantom pains — pains in the hand which he had lost, and which trouble him to this day.

'It is still strange to be able to feel my arm hurting even though I know perfectly well that it is no longer there,' he says.

At an RAF rehabilitation unit in Chessington he was fitted with an apparatus designed to enable him to write. It consisted of a thin metal rod attached by a harness to his right shoulder with a pen fixed at the other end. Peter's first letter with this device, written to his parents, began: 'This is not being written by a small child . . .'

The next step in preparing him for civilian life was arranged by a department of the Air Ministry which was concerned with the resettlement of Air Force personnel in need of help. Here it was decided that Peter should develop his voice as he might find a niche in broadcasting. For six months he was taken several times a week to London's Central School of Speech Training and Dramatic Art, after which he was auditioned at the BBC with the idea of becoming an announcer.

After a test, which involved reading the news in a small studio, Peter was told there was nothing wrong with his voice and diction but one thing had been overlooked when he had been trained with this job in mind — he was unable to operate switches when necessary and he could not handle the pages of a script. So sorry!

Peter was staying at his parents' home in Wallasey when he received an official letter telling him that he 'no longer fulfilled the physical requirements of the RAF'. Thus, at the age of twenty-four, he had to face the future on a 100% war disability pension of forty-five shillings a week plus allowances. Remembering that the BBC had told him that his voice at least was acceptable, Peter started to give elocution lessons locally.

One day in July, 1950, he set out for a walk and headed, for some reason he could not explain, towards the New Brighton pier. It was something that he normally had no interest in, never having visited it before, yet now he was drawn to it.

When he arrived at the pier he found that a show called 'Happy Time' was being performed in the open-air theatre. What stopped him in his tracks was the girl on the stage who was at that moment singing 'O My Beloved Father'. She radiated vitality and, on finishing her number, it seemed to the young man that she smiled at him when she vanished into the wings.

June Lynette, the singer with 'Happy Time', felt strangely excited as she walked off. In the audience she had glimpsed a young man with dark curly hair whose frank gaze had never left her; it was like a popular song about someone seeing a stranger across a crowded room. How could the sight of someone she had never exchanged a word with have such an effect on her?

'What's happened?' demanded the stage manager when he saw the expression on her face.

'I've just seen the man I am going to marry,' she replied.

It came as no surprise to June that Peter Spencer was waiting for her after the show.

He made some comment about her singing, asking who had taught her, and as she replied she noticed with a start that the right sleeve of his jacket was empty, the cuff tucked neatly into his pocket.

He glanced down at the case she was holding and apologized for not being able to carry it for her.

'I've lost both my arms,' he explained.

June did not embarrass him with an effusion of sympathy which she knew instinctively would strike the wrong note. Instead she merely said, 'How interesting.'

That evening Peter told her about his accident as they sat in the bar of the Grand Hotel.

When he had finished his story June told him that she did not feel at all sorry for him — and then asked if he wanted her to be.

'It's refreshing to meet someone who isn't,' he answered, realizing that it was a very unusual young woman sitting opposite him who was unconcernedly lifting a glass to his lips for him.

'I'd like to help you, though,' she continued. 'I like helping people.'

At this time Peter did not find his work — which mainly consisted of trying to teach children to say their vowels properly — fulfilling and his greatest consolation was the pleasure of June Lynette's company on various dates. When her parents came for a holiday in New Brighton he found to his relief that his disability appeared to make no difference to their attitude towards him.

When 'Happy Time' closed Peter was depressed at the thought that his happy time was over, and he felt both alarm and delight when she suggested

no man an island

a biography of Peter Spencer
by Eileen Waugh

foreword by Douglas Bader

24

that he should come and stay with her at her parents' house. He tried to point out the problems that could arise in their home on account of his disability, that he could not dress or shave himself. June told him not to worry, and she had already discussed it with her parents and her father would do what he could to help.

And so begain an idyllic six weeks, during which Peter met June's friends and went on numerous outings with her. It ended when she took a role in a pantomime in Dewsbury, Yorkshire, and Peter returned to Wallasey. After the pantomime June went to London to join Ralph Reader's National Light Opera Company, and when it moved to Blackpool Peter was able to stay at the British Limbless Ex-Servicemen's Association Hotel in order to be near her.

By now the young man was faced with a dilemma. He was deeply in love with June and wanted her to be his wife, but, if he felt so deeply for her, should he not consider her well being first and not expect her to face the problems that marriage to a man as disabled as himself would inevitably bring. Apart from anything else there was the question of how he could support her — and perhaps a family in the future — on his pension.

Finally the subject came up between them. Peter could not hide his feelings towards her but added that in his circumstances he had so little to offer. June ignored this and told him about her love for him, saying that it was wrong that they should continue to be apart.

'You mean you would marry me?' he asked.

'Of course. I was sent to marry and look after you. I have always known that.'

On 12 December, 1951, the couple were married in St Nicholas's Church in Wallasey. It had been decided that June should continue her stage career and, after a period with the National Light Opera Company in London, she and Peter were delighted when they were reunited through her taking part in a new show called 'Holiday Time' on the New Brighton pier.

One day Peter came across one of Ripley's 'Believe It or Not' cartoon features in a magazine. It described how a German named Erich Stegman, who was without use in his arms, had become a celebrated painter by holding a brush in his mouth.

It was a moment of inspiration for Peter.

'If he can do it, why can't I?' he thought.

Peter had taught himself to write by holding a pen in his mouth, which was more satisfactory than using the metal rod, before going on to use a typewriter with his feet, and so the prospect of painting with a brush handle clamped between his teeth was not as daunting as it might have been. With June's help a canvas was set up and he began what was to become his new career. He found that it took him longer than he expected, but as soon as the work was finished he launched into the next. Towards the end of the year he saw some Christmas cards which had been published by the Association of Mouth and Foot Painting Artists, and this gave him an idea as to how he might be able to channel his work. He submitted six paintings to the Association and waited eagerly for their verdict. When it came it was disappointing.

'Thank you for sending us samples of your work,' read the reply, 'but we regret that your paintings do not come up to the standard we require for publication.'

But if the Association did not want his work, at least they did not forget him. A few months later an invitation came to the Spencer's bungalow in Wallasey inviting him to attend an exhibition of members' paintings. He went with June and as they gazed at the paintings Peter felt overwhelmed by the quality of the work. At one point he got into conversation with a Dutch artist named Corry Riet who had been paralysed since the age of five.

'Have you met Erich Stegman our President?' she asked.

Peter shook his head.

'He is a wonderful man, so great an artist and so big a heart,' Corry enthused. 'He changed my life and he makes it possible for us to paint without

Peter autographs a copy of his book for HRH Prince Charles

worrying all the time where the money is coming from. Do come and meet him.'

Peter was led off to meet the man he had read about in the 'Believe It or Not' feature. Erich Stegman told him through an interpreter, 'Your work shows talent but the standard is not yet sufficiently high for us to accept for reproduction throughout the world on cards and calendars. I suggest that you attend art school and we will give you a scholarship to cover the cost of your tuition and materials.'

Thus Peter began a course at the Wallasey School of Art, and after his years of disappointment he felt that at last he was on his way. In May, 1958, he want to Paris at the invitation of the Association to attend an exhibition of Members' work which, now that he was studying to become a professional mouth painter himself, he looked at with new understanding.

He could imagine the countless hours that each artist had put in to perfect his or her skill acquired against varying backgrounds of disability. Now he could imagine the self discipline necessary to continue working when it would be so much easier to shelve it for a while, to keep the mind working when it felt that the body was in revolt. And now, seeing the outcome of such dedication, Peter was filled with a new determination that, come what may, one day his paintings would be hung among those of this wonderful band of artists.

June had been invited to accompany him to Paris but she remained in Wallasey as she was expecting the arrival of their first child. On the 27th of the month little Robin Spencer came into the world, and a dream which Peter once thought was lost forever came true. Having a son to provide for was yet another incentive for him, and he worked at his painting harder than ever before. Still-life studies, portraits and landscapes grew under his brush as he stood before his easel and sought to gain the required standard of proficiency, and with it the means to ensure a satisfactory life for his family. He achieved the role of bread-winner in 1959 when he and June attended a Mouth and Foot Painting Artists' conference in Edinburgh and he was officially welcomed as a new member.

The fulfilment of this ambition gave Peter the confidence to do other things which once would have seemed beyond his scope. In 1960 he stood for the local council, winning the Marlowe Ward and which he was to hold with increasing majority for the next fourteen years, after which he did not seek re-election. He served as President and Chairman of the Merseyside Branch of the British Limbless Ex-Servicemen's Association and as Chairman of the Wallasey Arts Society. He also discovered that he had a talent for giving amusing lectures and this became a regular aspect of his work. Later he took on the role of the Mouth and Foot Painting Artists' public relations officer which meant travelling to various parts of the world to promote the work of his fellow artists. Meanwhile their second child, Jill Rosemary, was born in 1962.

One thing that Peter had long missed was something that today most people take for granted — the independence which has been bestowed upon us by the motorcar. For a long time the idea of driving had been impossible but, like other impossible things in Peter's life, it became a reality when an automatic Mini had special controls fitted to enable him to drive using his feet only. He has derived a great deal of amusement from the expressions of people who see him piloting a car which appears to have lost its steering wheel!

Two events in the following years stand out in Peter's memory as special. The first was attending an exhibition of the work of Mouth and Foot Painting Artists in the House of Commons which had been instigated by Lynda Chalker, MP for Wallasey, in 1975. It was opened by Jack Ashley, MP, who, being totally deaf himself, has always been a champion of the disabled. The other event had a completely different setting.

Following an IRA bomb outrage in Caterham, Surrey when several Welsh Guardsmen lost limbs, the British Limbless Ex-Servicemen's Association and the Welsh Guards arranged an event which took place on 31 July 1976. Limbless men, helped and escorted by Welsh Guardsmen, went to Snowdonia in

North Wales and some walked and some went by train to the top of Snowdon. The day was honoured by the presence of the Colonel-in-Chief of the Welsh Guards, HRH the Prince of Wales who flew his own helicopter to join the men. At one stage he walked alongside Peter, chatting about aircraft and the difficulties of flying a helicopter in mountainous terrain such as Snowdonia. At the top of the mountain every man was presented to His Royal Highness, and holding the pen in his mouth, Peter autographed a copy of his biography *No Man An Island* which the Prince graciously accepted. To Peter there was something very symbolic about these disabled men making their way to the summit of the mountain.

In 1970 Peter Spencer's biography *No Man An Island* by Eileen Waugh had been published and became a best seller. In the foreword Douglas Bader, the famous wartime pilot who flew with artificial legs, wrote: 'This is a great story about a man who resolutely accepted Fate's challenge to go on living a normal life.' The title was based on the words of 17th century poet John Donne, and which had inspired Peter to write a song, part of which went:

No man an island
No man can be
Without another
To set him free . . .

Eight years later the book was translated into French and such was its impact there that among several French honours awarded him, the humanitarian society *Merite et Devouement Francais* presented him with *Le Croix de Commandeur* for 'exceptional services to humanity' which referred to the example he had given to others by the way he had shaped up to adversity.

In the Queen's Birthday Honours List of 1980 Peter was awarded the MBE. A few months later he, his wife and two children went to Buckingham Palace for the Investiture. Unable to shake hands, the Queen gently touched his left sleeve, then pinned the Award on his lapel and asked Peter one or two questions about his life. Peter reckoned this was the most memorable day of his life.

Peter's next award came two years later when he was made a Deputy Lieutenant of the County of Merseyside by the Lord Lieutenant, Wing Commander Kenneth M. Stoddart, AE. This is a high local Award given for services to the Community. His latest honour came on 30 May 1985 when he was made Life President of the Merseyside Branch of the British Limbless Ex-Servicemen's Association.

At his home in Wallasey, Peter Spencer continues his busy life with the help of June. He still works tirelessly on behalf of the Association of Mouth and Foot Painting Artists, and his painting continues. His son Robin is now a successful barrister in London while his daughter Jill follows her mother's interest in the stage as a dancer and a teacher of dancing. Like other disabled artists, his favourite subject relates to what was most important to him before his life was altered by disability. In his case it is aircraft, and this led to his being elected an Associate Member of the Guild of Aviation Artists.

'Quite Contented'

JOHN BUNCE

HAPPINESS for John Bunce is when he puts brush to paper on his magnetically controlled easel. 'To be paralysed through your neck sounds tragic,' he says. 'But you can learn to live with it if you are lucky enough to be able to take up something which completely fascinates you. In my case it was painting, which makes my disability become something in the distance — art becomes frontal.'

As to what he paints, whether it be in watercolour, oil or ink, he derives the same pleasure regardless of the subject.

'What I like painting is what I am doing at the time. I have no preference at all. I enjoy painting a woodland scene as much as a house, a seascape as much as a bowl of flowers. I suppose I am best on birds, perhaps because I do more birds than anything else.'

John had what he calls his 'silly accident' when he was doing his national service in Germany in 1952. He was a cook, a job which he enjoyed greatly, and his intention was to study to be a chef in the army so that when he came out he could run his own hotel.

One evening in his billet he was reaching up to put a book away on a shelf when he slipped. Unbeknown to him one of his fellow soldiers had pushed a box of tools under John's bed.

'When I felt myself falling I did what seemed the most practical and fell on to my bed, unaware of what was beneath it,' he says. 'I hit my head on the corner of the box and found that I was unable to move and my voice was reduced to a whisper.

'It's strange when something like that happens how you think of all sorts of stupid things. My first thought was, "Now I shall get out of the C.O.'s inspection tomorrow".'

When John was taken to a military hospital it was found that his fifth vertebra had been broken, with the result that he was paralysed from the neck down and could not speak. From Germay he was transferred to the spinal injury unit at Stoke Mandeville Hospital where he was given an intensive course of physiotherapy.

At that time in Stoke Mandeville John had the highest lesion of the vertebra that the doctors there had encountered and consequently he became what he described as 'something of a showpiece'. During this time he found that treatment did help a little; his speech returned as did a small amount of arm movement — enough for him to operate the small 'joystick' control of his electric wheelchair.

Two years is regarded as the limit for any improvement in such cases, and when this period was up John had to reconcile himself to the fact that for the rest of his life he would be paralysed and dependent on others helping him, a daunting prospect for a young man only just turned twenty. Yet all those who knew John were struck by his cheerful attitude, something which is still commented upon thirty years later.

'I suppose it may sound strange, but I am never depressed,' he says. 'I have a firm believe that the Lord takes care of us — that faith helps more than anything else, and the more you believe the better you feel. Problems I consider as testing periods.

'As a boy I was not especially religious although through singing in the choir I attended services regularly. It must have had its effect on me because when I was lying on my bed after my fall which — after my first thought

about missing inspection — I believed meant the end of the line, I got the chaps who were in the billet to say the Lord's Prayer with me. It was remarkable how much it helped me at that moment.'

For the last seven years John has been a member of the Christadelphian Church whose members arrange to take him to a service each Sunday.

'For me personally the Christadelphians have more to teach, though of course the general feeling is the same as in any other Christian belief.'

At the time John was in Stoke Mandeville it never occurred to him that the career of a professional artist lay ahead of him, especially when his first attempt, made to overcome tedium, was a 'painting-by-numbers' picture with a brush held between his teeth.

'I was bored out of my mind,' he explains, 'I could not sit down like some of the others and make baskets and bags and fluffy dolls and that sort of thing, so a member of the staff suggested out of desperation that I had a go at painting by numbers. Some sort of crude easel was rigged up, and I suppose everything started from there.' But when he left the hospital to be cared for by his mother and father this new hobby lapsed for a while.

'Then, to pass the time while I lay in bed, I used to read those little comic strip war books, and with a pencil I copied some of the pictures — a face or a tank — in the margin. I really enjoyed this, especially when my mother was out and I was alone in the house and I had to fill in time as best as I could.'

From these little drawings John went on to amuse himself by drawing on scrap paper though, as he now says, everything was out of proportion. Nevertheless, this sketching grew on him until one day a welfare officer mentioned an art competition which was currently being held, and suggested that John should enter one of his pencil drawings. To his surprise and delight he came first.

'That more than anything else gave me the encouragement to persevere,' he says. 'At that time I was afraid to use colour and I did everything in pencil. I suppose this is the logical way as I learnt to draw before I started painting,

33

and so I was able to get my details and shadows right quite naturally when I finally came to work with colour.'

When John finally made his first attempt with water colours he was propped up in bed — with the result that the coverlet was soon soaked with pale-coloured water.

'I had to work like a madman to catch up with it as it ran down the paper,' he says. 'Water seemed to be everywhere, but even so I did have some success — enough to make me want to continue.'

From time to time John had to go back to hospital and it was during a stay there that he learned that his father had contracted cancer.

'It was rather a grim time,' he recalls. 'I had split up with my wife — she had found someone else as so often happens when a husband or wife becomes disabled — and what I wanted most was to be close to where my Dad was. The only way I could do this was to go into a Cheshire Home in Wolverhampton where I was eight miles away from him which meant that I could see him quite frequently.'

After living at home John found it difficult at first to adjust to his new environment. His experience of the disabled had been confined to those who had suffered spinal problems similar to his own: now he was among people who had many kinds of disabilities and some of whom could communicate only with great difficulty. But before long he had adjusted to this new way of life and found that it suited him so well that he was to remain there seven years, then transferring to the Greenacres Cheshire Home in Sutton Coldfield where he has lived ever since.

'I would recommend this type of establishment to anyone with a serious disability,' he says. 'It doesn't restrict you; you are not a prisoner within your own four walls. Of course it is lovely to be at home; it's private and you have your relatives around you, but it doesn't give you very much scope. For one thing, whether you are trying to do artwork or writing or whatever, you get a fair amount of criticism and encouragement from the staff and visitors to the home.'

It was twelve years ago that it was suggested to John that he should get in contact with the Association of Mouth and Foot Painting Artists, an organisation which until then he had never heard of. The result was that he submitted some of his paintings and was invited to become a student member, becoming a full member in 1985.

'All that time was a period of learning which was very useful for me because I had never been taught anything about art,' he says. 'And I think the most important thing I learned was to be self critical. If I feel a painting I have worked on is not up to standard I have no hesitation in scrapping it.

'Six years ago I began to take on students. Today a couple of youngsters come for lessons at the weekends and I'm also helping a fellow patient to get started. What has been interesting is the amount of instruction I have gained for myself by teaching. It enables you to see your own work from a different angle.'

Today John works every day, health permitting. It takes him from ten days to three weeks to complete a picture which means that his time is fully taken up as he not only sends paintings for the Mouth and Foot Artists to publish as Christmas cards but he also has commissions to fulfill, and pictures to paint which he donates to charitable causes.

In his charity work he frequently gives demonstrations of mouth painting at church fetes and suchlike. He has appeared on television at least half a dozen times demonstrating his painting technique and taking part in chat shows, but what he enjoys most is when he is invited by headmasters to give talks at schools, though 'chat sessions' would probably be a better description.

'Usually I go for a whole morning or afternoon but sometimes when it is a large school I go for a whole day,' he explains. 'To win their interest I do an on-the-spot portrait of whichever pupil has a birthday that day, or whose birthday is closest. This is better than doing a flower study or something like that because the kids would think I had sketched it before I came to them. Then I tell them about being disabled, and about my work so that I try to get across to them that if a person is in a wheelchair he or she is approachable and not just a piece of flesh sitting there unable to communicate. I do think this approach gives youngsters a new understanding of the disabled.

'And when I give talks and demonstrations to adult groups, it shows them the reality behind the MFPA cards.'

Although John's cheerfulness is a byword in the Greenacres home, he has periods of ill health to contend with which halt his activities.

Like other disabled people he is susceptible to infection and 1984 was a hard year for him, illness making him spend a lot of it in hospital. During this period he found it a strain even to talk let alone to think about painting, but when he recovered the following year he made up for it by going on holiday to the south of France with two friends.

'We drove down to the Riviera and were based at St Maxime between St Tropez and St Raphael,' he says. 'Wonderful painting country and I really looked forward to painting landscapes down there as so many famous French artists have done, but I was to be disappointed. The first day I overdid the sunbathing with the result I got a badly burned lip which bled every time I held a brush in my mouth.'

One thing which made up for it was going into Spain to visit Salvador Dali's museum — John's favourite contemporary artist.

At the Greenacres Home John is able to have a room, whose glass walls overlook a garden, as his studio. Past paintings — some of them well known because they have been reproduced by the MFPA — hang on the walls while in the centre is a motorized easel which John designed himself. Electric motors raise and lower and alter the angle of tilt of the board — what is unique about it is the control. This consists of a magnet mounted on the tip of a mouth stick which, when placed against an appropriate square on a panel, controls the motors so precisely that with no more effort needed than when using a paint brush the artist is able to adjust his easel to his exact requirement. The only help that John requires is for someone to squeeze out oil paint from the tubes and to pin up his paper.

Another example of his ingenuity is a light metal frame which can be clamped to the armrests of his wheelchair. On this, at eye-level height, his Nikon camera can be mounted so that he can follow his interest in photography. He finds the only drawback to the system is that he has to take every picture from the same level, but he manages to compose each picture by manoeuvring his wheelchair. What he finds most useful about his photography is being able to capture a scene when on an outing in the countryside which he can later translate into a landscape painting.

John has one little quirk over his paintings which people find highly intriguing once they know about it. In every picture the artist incorporates a tiny rabbit, perhaps represented by merely an interplay of shadow and completely camouflaged unless you know what to look for. Hunt the rabbit becomes an absorbing puzzle for children who come to see his painting.

As John sits and paints in his studio he will tell you that he is 'quite contented' with his lot.

'Like anyone else I do have some regrets,' he says. 'One of these is that I have never met Arnulf Stegmann who founded the Mouth and Foot Paintings Artists partnership. That man did so much to help people like me around the world and through the MFPA his work continues. Although you can work on your own as a disabled artist, the Association gives you something to aim for — a real sense of purpose! — and another thing is that it enables you to meet orther artists who are in your situation. It is terribly important to be able to communicate with people who, through their own experience of disability, are on your wavelength.

'What I do feel really bitter about is when I see stories suggesting that the MFPA is out to benefit people other than its members. Such a story appeared in a Sunday newspaper last year, and I suppose some journalists will try and make a scandal out of anything. I just wished that when people read it they could understand what the MFPA means to people like me and my fellow artists who have gained independence and security for life from it.

'I have found nothing but good from the Association. It allows a disabled man or woman to do work which will support them in the only possible way he or she can, whereas normally they could not do anything but live off charity.'

AJBunce 4/5/84

The Penny Ballerina

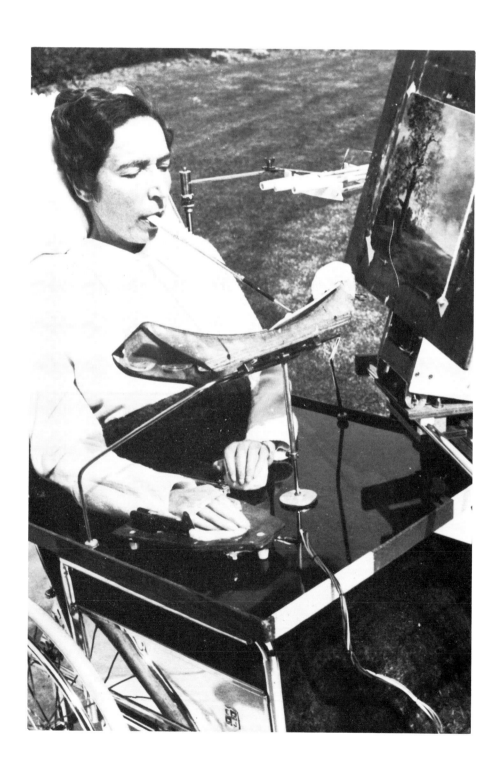

ELIZABETH TWISTINGTON HIGGINS

'If ever proof were needed that individuals are capable of making something of their lives in spite of the most adverse conditions, this story provides it.'

SO wrote HRH Prince Philip in a foreword to the biography of Elizabeth Twistington Higgins.* This story began when Elizabeth was aged fourteen and her brother Ian took her to Sadler's Wells Theatre in London to see the ballet *Les Sylphides.*

'It appealed to the very depths of my being,' she explained years later. The spontaneous effect upon her meant that from then on the only thing she wanted to do was to become a ballet dancer. To make such a decision is one thing, the stage-struck girl was to find that to put it into practice was a far more difficult matter. She discovered that she should have started serious training years earlier, and that she was too tall. Above all, there was the cautious attitude of her father who insisted that before any decision was taken about such a risky career, his daughter should complete her proper education.

Thomas Twistington Higgins was a pioneer of children's surgery who had met his wife Jessie during the First World War. He was serving in the RAMC and she was one of Queen Alexandra's Nursing Sisters. They were married in 1917 and now lived with their six children in a house in Highgate. He was a man who was very concerned for the welfare of his family, four of whom went into the medical profession.

During the summer holidays of 1939, the Second World War broke out and when the family returned from vacation Elizabeth found to her delight that her school had been evacuated, and the only school left open in Highgate was a dancing academy! With her sisters Brighid and Alison she was enrolled there and each day began with two hours of dancing lessons, after which came normal school lessons. By Christmas Elizabeth had matriculated, and once again she approached her father about ballet training. She quite expected to hear his reasoned arguments against the idea, but this time he merely said, 'If you insist on this crazy notion, you simply must get the best possible training so start at the top. Which is the top ballet school?'

'Sadler's Wells,' Elizabeth replied, hardly able to believe her father's words. But he meant them all right, because his next were, 'Right, if it's got to be — go there.'

Elizabeth wrote immediately asking for an audition, but when the time came she was embarrassed by lack of experience. Tears filled her eyes as she realized the gap between her ambition and ability, then to her amazement Ursula Morton, the school's principal, was not deterred by her poor performance — perhaps she sensed the girl's sense of determination which was to be such an important factor in her later life.

'Elizabeth, you've obviously got a good brain,' she said. 'Come for a three-month trial period.'

From then on it was sheer hard slogging as Elizabeth tried to make up for the years when she should have been training. When not at Sadler's Wells she practised at home, and before long her technique improved and her body became more supple with the endless exercises.

The happiness Elizabeth felt during this period came to an abrupt end

---

*The Dance Goes On, obtainable from the Association of Mouth and Foot Painting Artists.

when Ursula Morton told her as kindly as she could at the end of the probationary period that whe was physically unsuited to become a member of the company. As she spoke Elizabeth felt as though her heart was breaking, yet even at this point the idea of giving up did not cross her mind. She had set her heart on the stage and still felt that, by working hard, her ambition could be achieved.

Aware of her dedication to the dance, Ursula Morton recommended a school run by the Cone Sisters* where Elizabeth — to her disgust! — had to study all types of dancing including tap. Despite the fact that she could not concentrate fully upon ballet, she gained her Intermediate and Advanced Ballet certificates, and in 1945 won the highly prized Solo Seal.

Elizabeth became a full-time teacher at the school, but she still hankered to perform on the stage and so she decided to continue training with various famous teachers who included Stanislas Idzikowski, Vera Volkova, Lydia Sokolova and Anna Sevenskaya. It was at the conclusion of one of the latter's classes that her pupils were informed that there was to be an audition for a *corps de ballet* member in the musical *Song of Norway*. With a dozen other hopefuls, Elizabeth presented herself before Moyra Fraser, the leading dancer who explained that, since there was a lot of character and national dancing in the show, they would like the candidates to demonstrate the mazurka. How Elizabeth must have blessed Ursula Morton, who had taught her this difficult dance.

To her delight, Elizabeth was offered a contract — after years of practice, disappointment and determination, she had won through.

'It was thrilling to go through the stage door and up to the dressing room,' she recalls. 'The haunting smell of greasepaint, the suppressed excitement. This was the life I had wanted.'

When the show closed after fourteen months, Elizabeth did film and television work, took part in a Palladium pantomime, then successfully auditioned for the new Ivor Novello musical, *King's Rhapsody*.

But gradually Elizabeth found that she was suffering from a vague discontent.

---

*This establishment is known today as The Arts Educational Schools.

'I felt that being on the stage wasn't really doing much good for anybody other than myself,' she explains, 'and because I like children so much, I enquired around. It so happened that the management committee of Coram's Fields, a children's playground in Bloomsbury, London, was planning pre-school activities to give the local mothers a rest, so I started a music and movement class twice weekly, each session costing three old pence. It gave harassed mums a chance to rest in the playground or go shopping — play groups were not common in those days — and it gave the children a wonderful opportunity to let off steam.'

At the same time as Elizabeth began work with her pre-school group another Coram's Fields experiment was the Penny Concerts which, as the name suggests, were monthly concerts held on Saturday mornings where children were admitted for a penny to be entertained by musicians from the Royal Academy of Music. Violet Graham, of the Academy, had been running the scheme for twelve months when Elizabeth joined it to present dancing items, which she did for the next four years.

Before long Elizabeth's activities went beyond her music and movement classes and the Penny Concerts — in a corner of Coram's Playing Fields there was an open-air school for delicate children with chest and respiratory complaints, and the headmistress thought it would be a good thing is she ran a music and movement class for them as well. She persuaded the LCC to allow Elizabeth to become a visiting teacher for two mornings a week.

Prior to the school's birthday, word spread that Elizabeth was organizing a special celebration performance in which her friends from *King's Rhapsody* would take part. Costumes had been a problem until Ivor Novello heard about Elizabeth's spare-time activity and persuaded a theatrical costumier to provide them free. So many hundreds of eager children turned up at Coram's Fields that police had to be called to control the crowd, but the performance was a joyous success and Elizabeth earned the nickname of 'The Penny Ballerina'.

In 1951 the death of Ivor Novello stunned the company and although, true to tradition, the show went on, their inspiration seemed to have gone.

By now, Elizabeth realized she would get more satisfaction from teaching than performing, so she started dancing classes at the Art Workers' Guild Hall in London's Queen Square and many of her pupils came from her old classes at Coram Fields, children who could no longer go there because they were over five but who had loved their sessions with Elizabeth. The accent was now on proper dancing as opposed to music and movement, and she allowed those who could not afford the full fees to come at a reduced rate, because she felt they should be encouraged. Soon she found herself designing costumes, producing and choreographing ballets — and also helping at a school for the physcially handicapped.

Elizabeth had always loved needlework and when, in the Coronation Year of 1953, she was invited to assist with an exhibition of the royal coronation robes, to be held at St James's Palace, she jumped at the chance.

'The first night was televised with Richard Dimbleby,' Elizabeth recalls. 'It was opened by Queen Elizabeth the Queen Mother, who looked superb in her tiara and shimmering crinoline. I was thrilled and delighted to be presented to her. My days seemed very hectic, rushing between teaching, the palace and my home. I was always on the go.'

But Elizabeth was not to be on the go for much longer. Three weeks after the exhibition opened, while staying with her parents in Kent — they had moved there when her father had retired — she was taken ill. A local GP performed a lumbar puncture and decided that something was seriously wrong and, because there were no hospital beds available locally, Elizabeth was admitted to the National Hospital for Nervous Diseases in Queen Square. By an ironical coincidence the moment the ambulance brought her to the hospital entrance, her young pupils were arriving for their class in the Art Workers Guild Hall unaware of the plight of their Penny Ballerina.

It seemed to the staff that it was an extra cruelty that destiny should have chosen a ballet dancer — a person whose whole training and energy was directed to expressing herself with her body — to suffer complete paralysis.

Elizabeth had been stricken by poliomyelitis, which was one of the world's most feared diseases until the advent of Salk vaccine. Poliomyelitis attacks the nerve cells which control muscle movement but does not affect the sensory nerves, as Elizabeth found when she lay in the iron lung. Although she had completely lost the use of her limbs, she still felt pain in them.

As the dreary weeks passed the only improvement was a very slight movement in her right hand, otherwise she remained completely paralysed and it was only the effect of the iron lung inflating and deflating her lungs which kept her alive. Yet at first she did not realize the full impact of her illness.

When the news of Elizabeth's plight became known in the ballet world, everyone was stunned. Flowers arrived every day and, once visiting was permitted, she was never allowed to feel that she had been forgotten. Among the many outstanding tokens of love which stand out in her memory was a bridal bouquet from Dame Margot Fonteyn whose marriage took place at that time, and a posy of flowers from the children she had taught. Candles were lit for her by children from the local Roman Catholic church round the corner from Queen Square.

As there was little chance of Elizabeth's chest muscles ever working again, physiotherapists tried to restore some breathing capability by concentrating

on developing her neck muscles. They had hoped she would be able to use these muscles to draw air into her lungs.

When she first tried to breathe unaided, Elizabeth went blue almost immediately and twenty-seven months were to pass before she could breathe for three to four hours outside the machine. Every breath she took herself was, as it still is, the result of deliberate mental commands to the accessory breathing muscles in her neck (known as frog breathing), commands that must be given consciously no matter what else may be claiming her attention.

Although physiotherapists tried to develop movement in other parts of her body, there was only one tiny response — in her right arm. This inspired one of them to suspend a sling over Elizabeth's bed to support her arm so she could move it lightly to and fro. To give her an incentive to do this, one of the almoners brought in a typewriter. A stick was attached to Elizabeth's hand and the sling adjusted so she was able to press the keys with the stick. Elizabeth found it difficult to concentrate on two things at once — hitting the correct letter *and* breathing. It took years before she could master this.

It was a great milestone in her life when she had her first outing from hospital. She was lifted from the lung on to an operating theatre trolley, and

under the care of a doctor, a physiotherapist and two nurses, she was taken down in the lift and wheeled outside. Lying there and gazing up at the walls of the hospital, it seemed that, at every window, there were hands waving to her. Her temporary release meant a great deal to a lot of people.

When the time came for Elizabeth to move to another hospital Elizabeth was transferred to the Royal National Orthopaedic Hospital in Stanmore, Middlesex. At her first hospital, she had become involved and made friends with medical and nursing staff, all of whom had admired her courage. She had been accustomed to a room of her own where she could listen to music whenever she liked, and have visitors at any hour. Now the thought of being thrust into a new environment filled her with misgivings.

'Having been "specialled" until now, I was missing the seclusion of my room,' she said. 'I would have to get used to it, however, and looking back I realize that this toughening up process was vital to my rehabilitation. But at the time it seemed cruel, and I admit I was sorry for myself. I was made to feel aware of my helplessness.

'The physiotherapists at Stanmore were most understanding about my problem and depressions, but it took many years to fully accept the fact that I had been irrevocably immobilised. I had black days when I despaired of ever doing anything with my life.'

More than anything she wanted to keep her interests alive beyond the four walls of the ward and escape the long-term effects of hospitalization. Her sole aim in life was to be able to live at home again, and it seemed that in this she would be aided by a new type of breathing machine which had just been developed at Stanmore. Made mostly of light plastic, this portable cuirass-type respirator was, in effect, a wearable iron lung.

It was thanks to this invention that in the autumn of 1955 she was taken to stay at the home of her mother and father in Mongeham, Kent, where a room had been converted for her use. A physiotherapist and a district nurse made regular calls and when the latter, seeing Elizabeth's body for the first time, declared 'The Devil's own handiwork!' Elizabeth was able to laugh. The respirator worked so well that eventually she was able to travel round the Mediterranean by ship.

But sadly for Elizabeth the following winter was severe, and she lived in dread of storms bringing down electric cables and cutting off the power supply to her respirator pump. On several occasions this happened and her parents had to hurriedly get her out of the lung so that she could start her own conscious form of breathing. These tense incidents made Elizabeth realize that having her in their home was becoming too much for her parents, so after Christmas she was taken away by ambulance again — and for the next twelve years of her life she was to be admitted to as many different hospitals.

Psychologically she was at her lowest ebb in 1957 when she was in the British Polio Fellowship hostel. Her frustration was not helped by the fact that during the afternoons, there were no staff members on duty — so she could only gaze at the ceilings. She could not even turn the pages of her book.

Two paralysed fellow patients overcame the problem by mouth sticks. Until then, Elizabeth had rejected any suggestion of using an implement held in her mouth because she feared it would interfere with her breathing. Now, out of desperation, she tried a reading stick. It was difficult to manage, but she persevered and, to her delight, found she could still breathe with the stick clamped between her teeth.

After a great deal of practice and experimenting with different sticks, she was able to read a book without looking for help every few minutes. To Elizabeth it was an achievement of the greatest importance, as it was the first time in over four years that she could do anything for herself.

This led to Rosie, one of the Friends of the Hostel, suggesting Elizabeth try mouth painting and positioned a canvas board against a pile of books.

'What are you going to paint?' she asked, and Elizabeth thought she would try a landscape.

'We'll start with the sky,' Rosie enthused, and squeezed worms of paint on to the palette. Loading the brush, she then put the other end between her pupil's teeth. It waved wildly because she could not reach the canvas. As Rosie tried to adjust the books, they cascaded across the floor and paint spattered everywhere.

The effort had taken so much out of Elizabeth that she had to give up, but after a rest she was game to try again. Chewing viciously on the stem of the brush, she dabbed on the blue of the sky.

Slowly the paint covered the canvas — until Elizabeth bit right through the wood. When the board was moved back for her inspection she saw that her sky looked ghastly. But it had been fun, she would try again. At that point, she never dreamed her new hobby would be the key to her independence.

The dance goes on

THE LIFE AND ART OF
ELIZABETH TWISTINGTON HIGGINS MBE

by Marc Alexander
with a foreword by
HRH Prince Philip, Duke of Edinburgh

Elizabeth ended up in a room in the Dover Isolation Hospital and here she began painting lessons with a local art teacher named Rosemary Howard — an association which was to last for six years, continuing when it was necessary for Elizabeth to stay in hospital in Dover.

'It took Elizabeth nine months to master the technique of loading her brush with paint,' Rosemary explained. 'She cannot move her head forward very far so the board has to be moved into the orbit of her brush.

'Sometimes she would do a pleasing sketch and then — quite unexpectedly — jerk. The brush would slither down and all that effort would be wasted.'

Rosemary, her husband and friends, helped to improve Elizabeth's equipment and their excitement grew as they saw Elizabeth's talent start to develop, especially when it came to her ballet pictures.

'Obviously, inside herself she was dancing with those figures,' Rosemary said. 'When they were poised on one foot I felt she was somehow part of them; it was *her* arms that were extended, and *she* was on the stage under the lights.'

For Christmas 1958, Elizabeth's father used her painting of an arabesque figure in sepia as a Christmas card. This led to an interview with Roy Nash, a London journalist, and when the story appeared in an evening paper it was to lead to her first exhibition, held at the Dover School of Art, and further local library exhibitions in Canterbury and Folkestone. Her fame spread and, to Elizabeth's delight, fifty of her pictures were chosen to be displayed in coloured panels in the Queen's reception room during the Festival Ballet's Christmas season at the Royal Festival Hall. In 1961, the Matron of the Dover hospital asked Elizabeth if she would appear as the subject for TV's *This Is Your Life.* Normally the subjects of the show have no idea what is about to befall them until they are before the cameras, but in Elizabeth's case an exception was made because it was feared a sudden shock would make her forget to breath.

Elizabeth had dreaded the programme, but as familiar faces appeared from her past, she almost forgot the cameras. She saw the children she had taught, met her own dancing teachers, members of the musicals she had appeared in, Beryl Grey from the Royal Ballet, and members of her family who had given her such wonderful support all along.

After the broadcast there was such interest in Elizabeth's work that she soon had no paintings left to sell. She was delighted, but the old impossible dream of a home of her own remained. She could see no way to be entirely independent, but her few journeys to London by ambulance suggested she could be so for short periods. Why not an ambulance of her own?

The idea was fraught with problems but, helped by her father and loyal friends, a Bedford Utilicon was converted to her needs. The problems of chauffeurs was overcome by the members of the Deal Ambulance Service — later joined by some Trinity House pilots — who offered to drive her in their spare time.

Having her own transport strengthened Elizabeth's resolve to lead a more normal life. Somehow, she intended to achieve a home of her own, and the opportunity to do this came when she was asked to join the Association of Mouth and Foot Painting Artists.

Elizabeth said later, 'The contract seemed too good to be true, but after a lot of discussion I was convinced I should join. This decision marked the beginning of a more independent existence.'

Then began the long search for a house in which Elizabeth could spend her days even though she would have to return to a hospital at nights so that she could sleep in an iron lung. Finally her father located a suitable ground-floor flat in Walmer. It appeared to be ideal and within forty-eight hours it was purchased. Elizabeth found that the hardest part of getting going with her new life was getting the right type of help, but finally a rota of part-time helpers was organized, and at the same time she found new independence through an amazing piece of electronic equipment known as POSM, which stands for Patient Operated Selector Mechanism. As the years went on such equipment became more and more sophisticated. Today, mounted on Elizabeth's wheelchair and within easy reach of her mouth, is a slender plastic tube. By sucking or blowing into it, Elizabeth can activate the unit to perform many things: to summon her helper, open the front door, control lighting and heating, answer the telephone and so on.

In July 1966, Elizabeth's father, her constant supporter, died. For many weeks she found it impossible to paint and only the need for fulfilling orders for Christmas cards made her take up her brush holder again.

She worked hard to catch up with the backlog and her neck muscles became overtaxed. To her dismay, she began to lose control of her brush, and she was advised not to paint.

After some weeks the pain lessened, but when she experimented with a brush, paint spattered over the paper as it twitched out of control. A terrible fear grew within her. Was her career as an artist to end as had her dancing? When she was advised to take a break from painting for perhaps several years, she sought another outlet for her creativity and, with her arm slung below an overhead frame, she began to tap out a book of her experiences on an electric typewriter. Called *Still Life*, it was published in 1969 and it also became a talking book for the blind.

Gradually the use returned to Elizabeth's neck muscles and painting was possible again. But yet another world was opening to her — teaching ballet. This came about when her niece Penny asked Elizabeth to give her a ballet lesson. She agreed to try and, as there was no music, she began counting and singing to give Penny the rhythm. It left Elizabeth flushed and exhausted but it rekindled her old enthusiasm.

When Elizabeth's mother went to live with her daughter, Janet, Elizabeth moved to a house in Chelmsford, within easy reach of her sister. The Broom-

field Hospital agreed to have her as a night patient, and she remains so to this day.

Then Joan Weston, the honorary director and founder of the Chelmsford Ballet Company, asked Elizabeth if she would set a tarantella for eight girls. Elizabeth was aghast. It was one thing to give private tuition to her nieces but to teach eight strangers to perform publicly was another matter. Yet she had never refused a challenge. Teaching verbally was a great strain but somehow Elizabeth got over her ideas. The tarantella proved a great success and, for five years, Elizabeth was to be involved with the production of dances for the Chelmsford Ballet Company.

In 1971, something happened which was to fuse Elizabeth's lifetime of creative experience into a new and exciting whole. She was asked if she would arrange dance sequences for an experimental Eucharist in Chelmsford Cathedral. At first Elizabeth was against what seemed to be tampering with a sacred service, but the vicar was so enthusiastic that she came round to the idea that if it was done the right way dancing might have a place in the church.

The performance in the cathedral turned out to be highly moving. The effect on the congregation was profound, many were moved to tears, and from then on Elizabeth knew that she would be devoting a lot of her time to the development of liturgical ballet.

Invitations for Elizabeth to take the girls to other churches became so numerous that she formed her own group, The Chelmsford Dancers. For the next eleven years they performed all over the country, not only in the churches and cathedrals but for hospitals and charities, and twice in prisons.

Elizabeth designed their costumes.

'I was lucky to be able to put down on paper what I wanted and supervise them all the way through,' she said. 'And I knew from experience that a dancer performs better if she is aware that she is beautifully dressed.'

The process of creating a new ballet began with Elizabeth, like all choreographers, steeping herself in music.

'I usually played the music more than a hundred times,' she explains. 'But teaching is the hardest part of a new ballet. Often we really reached rock bottom because I tended to get exasperated when I couldn't explain well enough.

'What the public does not realize is the amount of team work that goes on backstage. So many people were involved apart from the dancers: dressmakers, drivers, helpers — and there is much to prepare ahead. The dancing area had to be measured, the surface of the floor examined, acoustics tested.'

Sheila Large, Elizabeth's assistant director, was a professional dancer before she came to Chelmsford and was a key figure in the group.

'What mystified many people was how Elizabeth managed to teach the most mobile of art forms from a wheelchair,' she says. 'No matter how well taught or classically trained, a new girl would find that she had to adapt to Elizabeth's individual style. But I had been with her so long that to follow her was second nature, and I was able to show the others exactly what she wanted.'

Another person without whose help the teaching of ballet would have been impossible was the inventor Reg Maling who pioneered POSM (Patient Operated Selector Mechanism) equipment for the disabled. He devised a control unit which allowed her to work a Uher tape recorder by blowing into a mouthpiece, and thus she as able to select, and when necessary repeat, musical passages for her pupils.

In 1977, the year of the Silver Jubilee, Elizabeth was awarded the order of the MBE, receiving this honour from Her Majesty the Queen, and what delighted Elizabeth most was that she had not been awarded her MBE for triumph over physical disability — *it was for her painting.*

An hour-long film, based on Elizabeth's biography *The Dance Goes On,* was shot in 1980. After tracing Elizabeth's career, it showed a day in her life during which she painted and put her dancers through a rehearsal. It ended with an inspired performance of The Chelmsford Dancers at All Souls Church in London's Langham Place. Rudolph Nureyev recorded the commentary, and after it had been shown on ITV as well as abroad the magazine *Films and Filming* named it the best documentary of the year.

For the next four years Elizabeth continued with her painting for the Association of Mouth and Foot Painting Artists and running the Chelmsford Dancers, and to its credit the Association did not object to the time taken over the latter — it was regarded as another form of presenting art.

In 1984 Elizabeth decided it was time to retire from ballet work. Several dancers could no longer take part because of career considerations, and with her dancers no longer able to get together enough for training and rehearsal Elizabeth said she could not let the company's standards drop — and the prospect of training a brand new group was too daunting.

'It is best to go out on a high,' Elizabeth said philosophically. The particular 'high' she referred to was the fact that her last pupil has just been accepted by the Royal Ballet School. This was a highly symbolic tribute to a teacher who long ago earned the nickname The Penny Ballerina for her work with children. And though the Chelmsford Dancers may be disbanded, in Elizabeth's paintings her dancers still appear to be filled with the essence of grace and movement.

'Forget the Wheelchair'

DERRICK VANDEK

IT was afternoon in a Manchester nightclub. On the stage a wrestling ring had been erected as wrestlers were to provide part of the evening's entertainment. Two of the burly contestants watched while another of the evening's performers placed a table in the centre of the ring and began to rehearse a balancing act. For a lot of the time he supported himself solely on his left arm and, with his body held straight, juggled hoops with his feet, played a harmonica in his right hand and performed the tricks which had made him one of the top acrobats in the country. Several other artistes joined the wrestlers in watching Derrick Vandek go through his paces. Then, when the finale was reached, he began jumping up and down on his table prior to somersaulting off it.

But when the sumersault came something went drastically wrong. The acrobat went straight through the ropes, one of which caught his foot and threw him so that he crashed to the floor. For a moment the onlookers waited, expecting him to climb to his feet, but as the seconds passed he remained prone.

'I just lay on the floor and a couple of wrestlers came across,' Derrick explains today. 'I heard one say, "Leave him lying, we'll have to get an ambulance." And I realized that I must have done something to myself. It seemed as though I could not feel my body at all and there was a lot of pain in my head. And, though I could speak, the words did not come out very well.

'The ambulance men lifted me on a stretcher very carefully and I was taken to the Hope Hospital in Salford. I remember a needle going into my arm and then I did not know anything until a day later when I came to and found myself strapped to a frame.'

In his fall on the stage Derrick had broken his neck.

'I was in traction — held completely immovable — for six weeks,' he recalls. 'And it was real torture. Every two hours I was turned over so that for a while I'd be face down and then I'd be looking up at the ceiling. But at that stage I never thought that it was the end of my career, I believed that I was going to make a comeback. The doctors did not tell me that I was paralysed for life, merely saying that it was "too early to say what the damage is". So I said to friends who visited me, "Give me a couple of months and I'll be back on the go again." Two months would go by and I'd be no better, so I'd say, "Give me another two months . . ." And I kept on saying it.'

At last Derrick had to accept that his show business days were over. Although he still had power in his shoulders and arms, he was paralysed from the chest down and he could not use his hands nor was there any feeling in them. It seemed the end of the road for the young man who had devoted his whole life to physical exercise.

Derrick Vandek was born in 1935 in the mining village of Cowden Beath in Dunfermline, Scotland. In those days there were seventeen pits in the area, and Derrick's father was a pit deputy. From his earliest days Derrick was crazy about sport, and at the age of seven took up gymnastics, often performing in local boys' clubs. And from an early age he wanted to get away from the village and see the outside world. So, when he got his National Service call-up papers in 1955, he decided that instead of joining the army for the usual two years, he would sign on for six. Soon after he had arrived at his basic training camp a physical training instructor saw him performing somersaults.

Derrick Vandek with Baroness Trumpington at an exhibition at The Royal Festival Hall

'I want you for the gymnastic team,' he said, and after Derrick had completed his ten weeks of 'square bashing' he was asked if he would like to have a try at becoming a P.T. instructor himself.

Nothing could have suited him better, and he was posted to Aldershot for six months' training, after which he got his first stripe — when he finally left the army he was an acting sergeant — and continued to go on advanced

courses. Apart from instructing the men, Derrick continued to train himself. He had found that he was best at parallel bars work, and from this he developed an acrobatic act in which a lot of the routine was done balancing on one arm. He was soon in great demand to perform at garden fetes and military tattoos.

At the same time Derrick began a career as a public entertainer in his off-duty time.

'While I was in the army I was also doing work in nightclubs and circuses,' he says. 'Sometimes I'd be asked to do a show for a week and I would when I could get seven days' leave. A high point came when I went to London to take part in the Mr Universe Show at the Victoria Palace, and following this I was offered more and more jobs. Because of this I decided to buy myself out of the army before my time was up, and become a professional acrobat.'

Derrick had been happily following his new career for six months when the accident during his rehearsal in Manchester cut it short. And though he buoyed himself up for a while with the belief that it could only be a matter of time before he was on the boards again, in the end he had to face the fact that for the rest of his life he would be paralysed.

After he was released from the frame to which he had been strapped he was transferred to a hospital in Edinbrugh so that he could be close to his wife who was living there with their two-year-old daughter. After eighteen months it was decided that as there was nothing more that could be done for him in hospital he could live at home, but soon he was to find that his troubles did not come singly.

'At that time my wife started to feel a bit off-colour, and to give her a spell from looking after me I would sometimes go for a fortnight's stay with my parents,' Derrick recalls. 'They had moved from Scotland to Mansfield in

Nottinghamshire after the mines round our home village closed. They were not only pleased to see me but also they knew it meant that my wife was getting a break.

'Then one day in Edinburgh the doctors told me that my wife only had twelve months to live. I had to keep this very quiet as she had no idea what was happening to her, and as I did not want her to be overtaxed with me, I told her that I was going to stay with my parents for a while.

'One evening my young brother Gordon took me to a nightclub to see some of my theatrical friends performing there. Suddenly I heard my name called over a loadspeaker. I was wanted urgently on the telephone but even before I was wheeled to it I knew what I was going to hear — that my wife was dead.'

It was decided that Derrick's little daughter should be looked after by her grandmother in Scotland, and Derrick would live with his parents in Mansfield, and now he asked himself what he was going to do — what could he do? — with the rest of his life. His disability was such that an ordinary job was out of the question, yet he could not bear the thought of sitting about in his wheelchair letting the days drift by. There *had* to be something that he could do . . .

The answer came from some old stage friends.

'Why don't you become an agent?' they asked. 'You could arrange our bookings with clubs, theatres and circuses.'

To Derrick it seemed a wonderful idea and his sixteen-year-old brother Gordon, a storeman with the National Coal Board, offered to help all he could.

'I was very lucky with my brother,' Derrick declared later. 'Without his support I certainly would not have been able to achieve so much. He gave me a lot of help.'

Derrick got a phone which he was able to operate himself, contacted show business people around the country and the new theatrical agency was in business. Soon he had an arrangement with a Continental agent who would send acts here while Derrick arranged for British artistes to appear in Europe. Later he also became the manager for two acrobatic acts. The work was ideal for him; he knew the business, liked the people and was independent.

For a while Gordon drove his disabled brother when it was necessary, but Derrick longed to be able to drive himself. As he still had movement in his arms, although not in his hands, a car was fitted with a special steering wheel but to his chagrin he found that his muscles had deteriorated to such a extent that he did not have enough strength to turn it. For the next six months he exercised with weights attached to his arms, with the result that he redeveloped his muscles enough to enable him to drive as easily, and for as long periods, as an able-bodied person. He has enjoyed driving ever since and has driven on the Continent when taking holidays there.

In 1970 something happened which, though it seemed trivial at the time, was to be of great significance to Derrick later on. He and his brother were on holiday in Majorca and one day, while he was on the beach, a lady came up to him and said, 'Excuse me, are you a painter?'

'No, I'm not,' replied Derrick in some surprise. 'Why should you think that?'

'It's just that I know someone disabled like you who paints with a brush held in his mouth. Have you ever tried painting?'

'No, though I enjoyed drawing when I was at school.'

The stranger said he ought to consider painting and she gave him the address of the disabled artist she knew, but Derrick soon forgot about it.

'After a few months I remembered what the lady had said and I got interested in the idea of painting,' Derrick says. 'I wrote to the artist and he wrote back explaining about the Association of Mouth and Foot Painting Artists, and I decided to see if I had any ability in that direction.' Derrick began with an oil painting of a lady in a crinoline which hangs to this day on his mother's wall because it was his first attempt. Today Derrick describes it as the sort of painting a child might have done, but it was not as bad as he had feared it might have been, and this encouraged him to continue. He soon improved his painting technique by lengthening the handles of his brushes so that he could paint with his face further away from the canvas and no longer needed to squint to see what he was doing.

'I found that I did better with the longer handled brushes, and I kept experimenting all the time,' he says. 'I did have a tendency to bite too hard on the handle — so much so that once I broke my false teeth.

'As I continued I found that I was best at scenes with trees or mountains, and I decided to concentrate on landscapes. I would drive into Sherwood Forest — a place I really love — and make sketches on the spot I would later turn into paintings.

'In 1972 I sent some of my work to the headquarters of the Association of Mouth and Foot Painters. For a while I heard nothing and I thought perhaps I was not good enough to be considered but finally a letter came telling me that the Association was interested in me as an artist and were prepared to take me on as a student.'

It was this letter which triggered Derrick into a new career. Over the past months painting had become the most important interest in his life, and now the student grant he would be receiving meant that he would be able to devote himself to it fulltime. He gave up his agency and worked towards the goal of full membership of the Association.

The year 1981 — the Year of the Disabled — was a memorable one for Derrick. It was the year he achieved full membership and it was also the year he married his second wife Kathleen.

The meeting was quite by chance.

'One day I drove my car to the local Post Office as I had to deliver a message to the postmaster,' Derrick recalls. 'I pulled up outside it and, not being able to get out by myself, I asked a passing lady if she would kindly ask the post-master to come out and see me. She did so. He came out and we exchanged a few words, after which he went in again and I saw that the lady was still there.

'"Is everything fixed up all right?" she inquired.

'"Fine, thank you," I replied. Seeing that she could be of no further help she was about to walk on.

'"Where are you going?" I asked. She told me that her home was up the hill, and I offered to give her a lift as that was the least I could do after the help that she had given me.

'I did take her home and it ended up with me inviting her to come on a picnic in my car. At first I don't think Kathy realized how disabled I was, but as we had more and more outings she got used to me, and things developed from there.'

At first the couple lived in a council house, but when Derrick became a full member of the Association he was able to afford a mortgage and they bought their own house in Skegby. Now Derrick and Kathleen spend their winters in an apartment in Spain to avoid the English winter which Derrick finds a hazard to his health.

'With the good weather there — no heating bills, for example — it is cheaper to be there than in England,' he says. 'And the flat has a big balcony on which I can sit and paint happily in the sunshine, which I find very important towards keeping me fit. It is an ideal situation for an artist.'

Derrick had his first holiday in Spain in the sixties.

'People used to laugh at the idea of me taking a foreign holiday when I first suggested it, and I was told about all the difficulties I would have because of being in a wheelchair,' he says. 'But I was determined to go and I used to say "Forget the wheelchair!" And somehow I managed it.'

Derrick believes that he was lucky that when he was young he had a disciplined upbringing which, combined with his army training, helped him to face life after he was disabled. Now, although he still misses his life on the stage, he does not feel saddened when he sees someone performing an acrobatic act on the television.

'I appreciate the effort that goes into it,' he says. 'I realize that it might have taken the performer a couple of years just to perfect one trick.' Obviously the patience he had to learn when he worked up his own act stood

him in good stead when he was endeavouring to become a professional painter with a mouth-held brush.

'It's funny how your past experiences help you later in life,' he says. 'I think I first got a feel for landscape when I was a boy in Scotland and loved to wander in the woods and go to Boy Scout camps. And I have been told that a theatrical aspect comes through in my paintings. At an exhibition a man came up to me and asked, "Were you ever in show business?" I asked him what made him say that, and he explained that the way I used light and shade had a hint of stage lighting about it.'

The Quality of
Acceptance

CHARLES FOWLER

CHARLES Fowler lost both his arms in a railway accident at the age of eighteen. On the Tuesday before the accident he had a dream in which he saw himself on a railway track, covered in blood. Over the image of his dream appeared the words 'beware of Wednesday'. He was exceptionally careful alighting from the train on the Wednesday, but on Thursday, being in a hurry to meet a friend, he opened the door of the railway carriage too quickly, slipped and fell between the platform and the line. The train wheels amputated his arms above the elbows.

'There is no doubt that I did dream my accident,' Charles says today. 'I have had many "foretelling" dreams since then, one example being when the husband of one of my friends died. I dreamt that he had a dark brown walking stick with a silver top. I telephoned my friend and described it to her and she said "Oh yes, there it is, by the side of his chair." '

Perhaps because of his unusual experiences there is an element of fatalism in his philosophical makeup. Charles is interested too in aspects of Spritualism.

Charles Fowler was born in Chelsea where he had a very happy homelife, his easy-going nature protecting him against the problems which threaten some only children. He enjoyed school where his favourite subjects were geography, history and art, a subject in which he won several prizes which encourged him to consider the possibility of getting a place in an art school. In the end he yielded to practical considerations and sat for a London Chamber of Commerce examination. Having passed his exams, Charles became a clerk at the age of seventeen. A year later he had his accident and his career in the linseed oil trade was at an end.

Charles was to remain in hospital for two months, during which time he attempted to come to terms with his new circumstances.

'It is a lifetime ago and I hardly ever think about it now,' he says today. 'But I remember I found it less difficult than you might imagine. It was a great nuisance of course, but the point was I was very young and therefore it was much more easy for me to adapt than if I had been twenty-five or thirty. And I was helped by the sheer sense of not worrying — I had the quality of acceptance, as indeed most disabled people have too.'

But if Charles was prepared to accept the fact that he had had both arms amputated, it did not mean that he was going to meekly accept the fact of his disability.

'I think one of the best things I ever did was to say to myself: "When I can leave hospital I'm not going to go home in a car, I'm going to walk back." ' And walk back he did to his parents' Wimbledon home.

It was after his return from hospital that Charles felt an urge to paint so he took to holding a brush in his mouth.

'There was no other way of doing it,' he explains. 'And even in the beginning I had very little difficulty with the method. As I said, I was very adaptable then. And compared with so many mouth and foot artists, I am extremely lucky in that I do not have a breathing problem and I can walk about.'

The subject for Charles' first attempt as a mouth painter was a tulip in a vase. Soon afterwards he painted a May tree in blossom. This proved to be a very popular picture with friends and acquaintances and so many offered to buy it that Charles set up a production line of May tree studies with seven paintings being worked on simultaneously. The fact that he could earn money from his art, even though it had been produced by a brush clamped between his teeth, was a great encouragement and Charles decided to develop his talent. To this end he began lessons in the studio of a professional artist in Tulse Hill, which meant a rail journey from Wimbledon. Despite his traumatic experience at the Wimbledon Station, Charles was determined to go backwards and forwards alone, and developed a technique for opening carriage doors with his foot.

By this time he had had artificial arms fitted at Queen Mary's Hospital, Roehampton, and found that these limbs greatly increased his independence. 'I am fortunate in being able to eat with a specially designed fork, to shave, to open doors, to play chess and to perform other functions, besides possessing two useful defensive weapons!' he says.

It was then decided that Charles should attend an art school. 'I rather wondered how I would be received at my first class,' he says, 'but I found it to be much better than I expected. When I was sent to the life room I picked up a pencil in my teeth to start drawing and everybody looked round — and after that I was ignored as an oddity and accepted as a student who could draw.'

61

When Charles had attended art school for four years, he was awarded the Ministry of Education's Award of High Merit, with the second highest award in the country for life painting. After this he won an Exhibition Scholarship to the Royal College of Art where he studied for a further four years, taking a Continuation Scholarship and gaining his Diploma. But when college life came to its conclusion, Charles had to think seriously about making a living out of art which is one of the hardest professions in which to get established. Although his work was exhibited in various galleries, including those of the Royal Academy, the Royal Society of British Artists and the Royal Society of Painting in Water Colour, Charles wanted the security of a regular income.

The artist with whom he had had his first lessons at Tulse Hill was now the Principal of Farnham School of Art and, having followed Charles' progress over the years, now offered him the post of teaching Still Life one day a week.

When he introduced the new lecturer to his class, the principal told them 'not to be nervous with Mr Fowler', adding that it would be a kindness if someone would light a cigarette for him if he needed it. Charles then went to work, and half way through he asked a student to take a cigarette from the packet in his pocket and give him a light when he had got it between his lips. Feeling more relaxed, Charles continued the lesson until the cigarette was burning uncomfortably close to his mouth. Without thinking he flicked it into a wastepaper basket with a jerk of his head. The class watched wide-eyed as the basket, which contained some turpentine-soaked waste, erupted with a gush of flame — a spectacular way of beginning a teaching career, Charles decided.

Apart from this conflagration he found that he enjoyed lecturing and would like to do more of it. He visited various art schools where he did his best to convince those in charge that his disability was no handicap when it came to imparting knowledge. As a result he was given work as an evening lecturer at Richmond Institute. This situation was ideal because it left him time for his own painting, and at the same time provided him with an absorbing interest as he came to realize how much teaching meant to him. And the fact that he had found his real vocation was proved a few years later when he was invited to become lecturer in charge of the Richmond Institute's art departmnet, and then its head, a post which he held for the next fifteen years. During that time the number of student enrolments in his care rose from eight hundred to two thousand.

'I am lucky in that I still have many friends from those days,' Charles says. 'I had a staff of four full-time lecturers and twenty part-timers, and I am still in touch with many of them.'

In 1963 Charles' mother died, followed by his father two years later, and he had to face the prospect of life on his own which can be very daunting for the disabled. What he really needed was someone to keep house for him and attend to his needs, and he decided to go to the Citizens' Advice Bureau in the hope that they could put him in touch with someone suitable. By a happy coincidence a lady who had been recently widowed went to the same bureau the next day to say that, now she was on her own, she wanted to get involved in helping someone in need of assistance. The secretary of the Bureau introduced them and was gratified to see that they took to each other, and the outcome of the meeting was that Charles found an ideal person to keep house for him.

'I was so lucky to find her,' Charles says. 'She is one of the most unselfish and helpful people I have met.'

During college vacations Charles travelled extensively, and still does, particularly in remote and unspoilt spots which are reflected in his painting.

'I am an Atlantic rather than a Mediterranean person,' he explains. 'I love feeling the power of the wind and watching the movement of the sea.' One of his favourite places is Sark in the Channel Islands. When he is on painting trips, Charles sometimes makes pencil sketches on the spot.

'If there's nobody around I like to paint on the spot,' he adds. 'It's strange that, after all this time, I get a little unsure when I know there are people about watching me. I know it's silly but I'm not like Arnulf Stegman who couldn't care less who was watching him. I was lucky enough to meet him several times — what a wonderful man he was.'

Charles retired from college work in 1975, and it was then that a friend suggested that he should get in contact with the Association of Mouth and Foot Artists, an organisation of which he had not heard. Intrigued, he visited the Association's office just north of Hyde Park where the work was explained to him. He was given a copy of Peter Spencer's biography *No Man an Island* which made him all the more interested in the Association, so much so that he submitted eight water colours. These were of such a high standard that he was given full membership immediately.

Today Charles Fowler is as busy as ever, painting almost every morning and lecturing on the work of the Association. And it is he who arranged many of the exhibitions of the members' work which are held on average twice a year.

Apart from work, Charles continued to travel in order to get new subjects. He enjoys listening to music — Mozart always, but he is catholic in his musical tastes.

'I have many interests outside painting, chess being one of my time consuming hobbies and I enjoy the study of history, geography and ornithology. I like good food and wine and perhaps would have liked to cook.'

'Although I am disabled, as far as possible I refuse to admit it and do not like the word, though it is difficult to find a satisfactory alternative. Handicapped people generally are subject to a great deal of misplaced sympathy. When this sympathy and help is understanding and unobtrusive it is welcomed gratefully. When it is sentimental and sensational it is not.

'But I remember, when travelling through France with a friend, how the words "sentimental" and "sensational" took on a different meaning. We stopped at a lovely hotel on the upper Seine, ate a very good dinner at the end of which the proprietor came to our table and asked how I lost my arms. Before I could reply, my friend stated, to my horror, that I had been a Captain of tanks and had been blown up by a mine in Italy during the war.

' "How very sad," said the patron.

' "Not at all," I replied. "One has love, the beauty of nature, and there is always cognac."

'He promptly brought a bottle which he helped me to drink, eventually becoming sentimental, and the result the next morning for me anyway was certainly sensational!

'But, more seriously, a recent talk of mine on the Association of Mouth and Foot Painting Artists illustrates the best kind of aid. I had dinner beforehand, where the help given to me was unobtrusive and sincere and, at the conclusion of the film show, the vote of thanks was given with admiration and genuine feeling and without fuss. A cheque from the sale of cards was placed discreetly in my pocket as I left.

'The M.F.P.A., a remarkable co-operative of severely disabled artists, exists solely because of interest, admiration and financial help given by such people all over the world.'

'I'm Glad That I
Survived'

PAUL DRIVER

FOR as long as he could remember Paul Driver had been in love with the sea, thus it came as no surprise to his parents when in 1944 he volunteered to join the navy. He was then eighteen and training to be a quantity surveyor, and it was with great anticipation that he looked forward to exchanging a tedious office job for the rolling deck of one of His Majesty's ships of war.

But instead of an admiralty notification to report to a naval training establishment, Paul received a letter from the Ministry of Labour, and his heart sank when he realized that he had been chosen to become what was known then as a Bevin Boy. It referred to a scheme introduced the previous year by Ernest Bevin, then Minister of Labour, to keep up the workforce in Britain's coalfields. To begin with men who were called up were offered the opportunity of working in the pits rather than joining the services but the response to this invitation was so poor that a ballot system was introduced whereby one in five recruits was drafted into mining work.

Paul went to Creswell Colliery where he was given a month's training and then sent to the small mining village of Eastwood on the Derbyshire border. To Paul, who had an ambition to become an author, its main interest was that it was the birthplace of D.H. Lawrence. Some of the older miners with whom Paul worked could remember Lawrence's father who they declared had been treated harshly by his celebrated son.

Paul worked underground 'ganging' or driving pit ponies, and was lodged in a spartan hostel with other Bevin Boys.

'The life had something of the army and something of university about it, with endless discussions on politics, philisophy and religion — but especially politics,' Paul recalls today. 'I had been interested in writing for some time and it seemed to me that here was a vein of material rich enough for any would-be writer. I tried, but without success. Nevertheless, after three years in the hostel my acquaintance with books, ideas and people had broadened considerably, and some of the friendships I formed then have lasted until today. At weekends I enjoyed cycling to the countryside around Nottingham or the Peak District, and in retrospect those years had more of pleasure than of discomfort.'

When Paul was released into the post-war world he was faced, like so many others, with the problem of trying to decide what he wanted to do with his life.

'I left the pit completely undecided, but not being rich enough to ponder the subject too long, I took a job as a clerk in a city office and spent my evenings at night school studying for matriculation,' he says. 'The job was boring beyond belief. The firm dealt with the bunkering of ships which involved endless pieces of pink paper all looking alike. I learned the name of every oil-burning ship then in the British Merchant Marine, and how to calculate instantly a commission of one shilling and three pence on any given number of tons — and decided it was time to leave!'

Paul returned to quantity surveying with the London County Council Housing Department.

'My twenties were good years,' he says. 'At the beginning I had little money but the things I liked doing — cycling, walking, staying at youth hostels — were not expensive. Alone, or with my younger brother, I covered a large part of England on my bicycle. With a friend from my mining days I

visited France and Scotland, and there were long walking tours in Wales, Cornwall and the Lake District.

'I learned to sail a dinghy on the River Blackwater and spent many holidays on the Norfolk Broads. Sailing was to me the purest pleasure I knew, whether I was trying in a dinghy to coax steerage way from an almost non-existent breeze, or hanging on to the shuddering tiller of a thirty-footer with the sails full and the wash rushing past the hull. I often thought of my boyhood when, passionately fond of the sea even then, I longed to sail in a windjammer.

'I joined the Territorials and saw something of army life. Somewhat reluctantly I acquired a motorcycle. It was quicker for getting to work and increased my range at weekends, and when I got my own boat — as I was determined to do — I would need it to reach the moorings.

'I had girlfriends, but nothing serious as I had no wish to settle down. Once qualified I could go abroad, for there were still plenty of British colonies with public works departments needing quantity surveyors. Meanwhile there was always something new to plan for. I had a long list of things I still wanted to do — walk along Hadrian's Wall and the length of the Pennine Way, to sail on the Dutch canals and to visit Norway. I satisfied my desire to write by keeping detailed journals of my travels, with extravagent word pictures of scenery.'

Paul left the LCC to work in a private firm which had opened a new office in Leeds and, with the Pennines and the Yorkshire Moors, Paul found a whole new countryside to explore.

It is ironic that several artists written up in this book enjoyed more than average physical activity before being smitten with disability, and so it was in the case of Paul Driver. His sailing and rambling ended in November, 1955, when he became one of the victims of the poliomyelitis epidemic which had been so virulent in Britain that year.

At first he believed he had nothing worse than 'flu, but when he collapsed on his bed and could no longer hold up his head his landlady called a doctor and within an hour he was admitted to the Seacroft Hospital on the edge of Leeds. Already he was having difficulty in breathing and he knew that he had contracted polio when a doctor told him, 'We are going to put you in a chest box', meaning an iron lung.

For the next few days he was hardly aware of what was happening about him; he was left with a confused recollection of faces close to his, and one of the most frightening moments came when he was slid on a stretcher so that nurses could attend to him. They had to work fast because at that time he could only survive for a minute without the help of the breathing machine, and just as he was being put back into it a hot water bottle fell under his feet and prevented the lung closing properly.

As Paul blacked out through lack of Oxygen one of the nurses dived forward and managed to pull the hot water bottle clear and the rubber collar was hastily sealed round his neck. The changing air pressures in the machine got his lungs working again and he recovered consciousness. But so poor was Paul's prognosis that one of the doctors later said to the nurse who had freed the lung in the nick of time, 'Why did you bother?'

For a whole year Paul remained in the iron lung, during which time he tried to pass some of the long hours by reading. This was done by the book being opened on a glass shelf fixed above his face. The problem was waiting for someone to turn the page when he came to the end of it. It was frustrating to have to wait for some well-disposed passerby to do it for him, and one answer to this was to read as many books as the shelf would hold at the same time. Even better, he found, was to have an Ordnance Survey map placed above him. In his imagination he could follow the paths he had once trod, translating the printed symbols into vivid pieces of landscape.

While he was in the lung Paul made better progress than had originally been thought possible and by using his throat muscles to breathe he was able to remain out of the iron lung for periods up to eight hours.

In explaining the method by which he was able to breath independently again, Paul says, 'I normally breathe with the remaining muscles in the front and side of my neck — the muscles that you would use if you were taking an extra deep breath. Glossopharengeal breathing (frog breathing) is a separate process. It consists of trapping small amounts of air with the soft palate, forcing it down into the lungs and holding it there by closing the larynx, then repeating the process several times so the chest is pumped up rather like a bicycle tyre. It is difficult to describe and difficult to understand. I did not learn to frog breathe — I began doing it quite unconsciously when I was first learning to breathe outside the lung. Other people I know also began to do this spontaneously. I do not depend on frog-breathing (although I know several people who do) but use it when I need a bit more breath or when I need an extra deep breath such as when I cough.'

Later Paul was moved to Pinderfields Orthopaedic Hospital where he was given special exercises. Here a rod with a rubber tip was attached to a head harness which enabled him to turn the pages of his book — a simple device which to his joy enabled him to turn the pages of his book himself.

Eighteen months after he had been rushed to hospital Paul was transferred to the Western Hospital in Fulham, London, so that he would be close

to his mother and father. By now the iron lung had been replaced by an ordinary bed in which he could sleep at night wearing a portable respirator. During the day he was dressed and allowed to sit up in a wheelchair, and when his brother got married in the summer of 1957 he was considered well enough to go to the wedding.

When Paul had been first stricken by polio he had been almost completely paralysed but thanks to physiotherapy more movement returned to his legs and feet. This was encouraging, though he had to face the fact that he would not be able to use his arms again. In trying to decide what the future might hold for him, Paul's ambition to be an author was revived and he experimented with a Biro held by the toes of his right foot as a method of writing. Despite all his attempts, the ballpoint would not stay in position until a visiting art teacher fixed it to a small bobbin which held it more firmly between the first and second toe.

Although the pen now stayed in place, Paul found that when he crossed his right leg over his left and tried to make letters on a pad propped in position on his bed it was far harder than he had imagined. Downstrokes were not such a problem but controlling the upstrokes caused him great difficulty.

It was obvious that this method was not going to be the answer to Paul's need to write, and a typewriter was provided which he managed to use successfully by hiting the keys with a short piece of dowel taped to his big toe.

The next innovation was a piece of equipment which enabled him to feed himself.

'By a strange coincidence it was invented in New Zealand for a man who not only had the same problem as me but also the same surname — Driver,' Paul says. 'Jim Driver, who I later learned was already a member of the Association of Mouth and Foot Painting Artists, had a "Distaff" gadget invented for him by an engineer named Taff — hence the name "Distaff". It consisted of a thin metal arm mounted on a metal tube and which the user could operate by means of a foot pedal. I cannot tell you what a great delight it was to be able to sit at a dining table and eat under my own steam after having been fed by nurses for so long.'

Now that he could type, Paul pressed on with his efforts to become an author, taking a correspondence course in writing. But he also found a new hobby in painting. Although a pen held between the toes had not been a success, he discovered that he could manage a paint brush quite well and the art teacher who had provided him with the bobbin holder now encouraged him to draw and then put colour on his drawings. His first efforts were understandably crude, but he soon made such progress that when an art exhibition was held at a local library the hospital chaplain took along several of Paul's paintings to be exhibited. The fact that they had been painted by foot appeared in a newspaper report which found its way to the Association of Mouth and Foot Painting Artists who — always on the look out for suitable talent to foster — asked Paul to submit samples of his work to them.

'I did not take up the offer because I felt my work was too amateurish and regarded it as nothing more than a hobby,' Paul says. 'I still saw myself as a budding writer.'

At the end of 1960 Paul went for a year to the Mary Marlborough Lodge, the new Nuffield Orthopaedic Centre in Oxford which had been set up to assist the disabled to make the most of what movement was left to them. It was here that Paul learnt to control an electric wheelchair which was adapted to foot control. He also found that he could earn money again after half a decade by typing labels for a local publisher, and later he typed typescripts of translations of Russian mathematical books. In order to improve his efficiency in this field he went to Russian classes with a staff member and, as his typewriter did not have Russian letters, he wrote them in where necessary with a pen held with his toes. This demonstrated how greatly his foot control had improved, especially as he no longer needed to use the bobbin to hold the pen.

After a year at the Mary Marlborough Lodge, Paul went to live near his parents at the Athol House Cheshire Home in Upper Norwood, and here with a fellow resident he organized a typing and duplicating service, pressing other residents into service as the volume of work increased. The proceeds from this enterprise went in part to run an ambulance which, driven by a rota of volunteers, was used for outings, and to provide other amentities for the home.

By now Paul realized that his future did not lie in the world of literature but, as though to compensate for this, he had to admit to himself that his painting had progressed remarkably. Until then it had been a pleasant hobby; now it was something much more serious and, using photographs to ensure that he got the details right, he set about painting a series of water colours of Thames sailing barges, those amazing coastal sailing craft which had fascinated him since childhood. Once more the Mouth and Foot Artists came into his life when he met two of its members and, remembering the Association's earlier interest in him, he sent several paintings for consideration by the Association's panel with the result that he was made a student member early in 1966.

Now that he was accepted by the Association he was able to afford to have private tuition and he embarked upon his new career with his usual thoroughness and enthusiasm. He studied composition and painting techniques — transferring like many disabled artists from water colours to oils — and instead of relying on photographs he began painting from life. In order to be able to compare his work with able bodied students he joined a portrait class organized by an evening institute.

In the same year that he joined the Mouth and Foot Painting Artists, the health authorities provided Paul with an electric invalid tricycle which could be operated by foot control and which had a range of twenty-five miles. This added a new dimension to his life; he was able to explore again — Richmond Park, the byways of London and above all the Thames-side which provided inspiration for his paintings which, due to his lifelong love of water and boats, depicted sailing craft ranging from great Tudor warships to modern yachts with straining sails. An extra pleasure was to be able to go to sea again in a pleasurecraft specially fitted to take a number of disabled people in wheelchairs.

After five years as a student Paul became a full member of the Association and from then on was financially independent and able to pay his own fees at Athol House.

In 1975 he married a girl from Switzerland who had worked at Athol House some years before and had kept in touch with the home. They moved into a flat in a block built by the GLC to be accessible to wheelchairs, and now they have two sons, born in 1977 and 1979. Family holidays spent in Switzerland with Paul's wife's mother explain the alpine scenes which Paul paints along with his famous seascapes.

A room in the Drivers' flat has been turned into Paul's studio. Its large window overlooks a grassy garden and trees whose summer foliage gives one the illusion of being in the countryside. The walls are hung with paintings; there are piles of reference books so that Paul can ensure the details of his bygone ships are accurate, and there is an exciting hint of turpentine and drying oils.

Paul's method of working is to have an extra large palette on the floor close to his easel which is angled almost at floor level. And so that he does not need to depend on a helper to unscrew his tubes of paint, he devised a simple but effective way of keeping them so that he can squeeze the colour out with his toes whenever he wants to. This is done by keeping the uncapped tubes upside down in small jars of water which prevent them from drying out and becoming hard, and which are easily available to be picked out by his toes.

Paul — the only foot-painting member of the Association in Britain — paints by sitting in a wheelchair from which the footrests have been removed so that he can use his feet to manoeuvre easily in front of his canvas. He works nearly every day on his beloved marine subjects, and also on landscapes and flower studies which as Christmas and greeting cards are now well known around the world.

In the early days of his illness, when his life was dependent upon the iron lung in which he was encased, Paul's future seemed to be blank. The prospect that one day he would become a professional artist, get married and have two sons would have seemed beyond belief, yet through his extraordinary determination, firstly to learn to breathe again and secondly to make himself proficient in painting, these things came about. Once when commenting upon the path his life has taken, he has been quoted as saying in his typically cool way, 'I'm glad that I survived.'

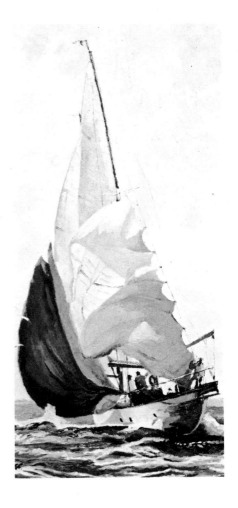

The Epitome of
Contentment

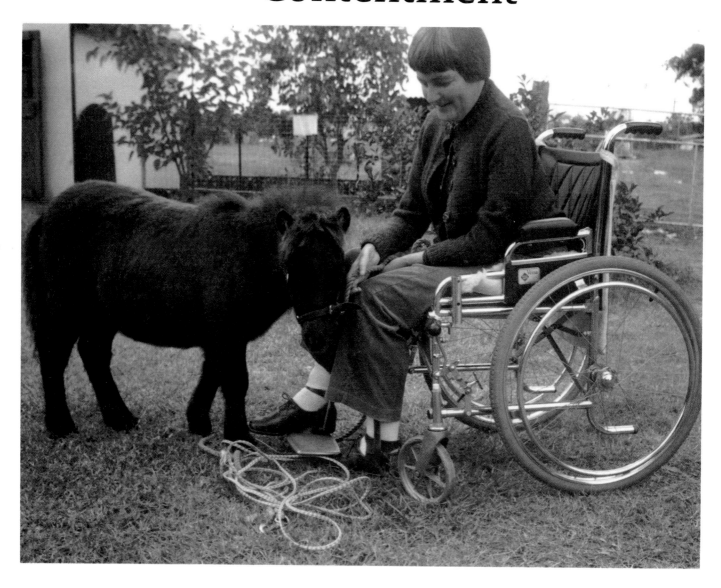

MARGARET GREIG

For I have learned in whatsoever state I am, therewith to be content. —
Philippians 4:11

WHATEVER the situation, words to fit it are sure to be found in the
Bible, and in this case they could not be more appropriate. The
verse is pinned up on the wall of a large and airy studio which was
specially built for an artist who has learned to be content despite the fact
that during her teenage years and adult life she has been quadriplegic. A
recent newspaper story on her described her as 'the epitome of contentment'.

Today such descriptions of the disabled are expected. Because so many
have put on a brave face for the world, cracked jokes with those who help
them and resolutely resisted the temptation to bewail their fate, the myth
that in some way physical disability bestows cheerfulness has grown.

In fact, acceptance of disability is one of the hardest things which some
people are called upon to undergo, and if anyone does not realize this they
should reflect upon the fact that among the intriguing paraphernalia of Margaret Greig's studio is a memento from her childhood — a riding saddle.

She will tell you it is there because it is a reminder of home, but one has
only to look at her paintings to realize it is much more than that.

It is a symbol of a lost way of life.

And perhaps when she raises her eyes from her easel and regards this
single souvenir from her early past, it takes her back to the beautiful countryside of Moruya on the south coast of New South Wales, great farming
country with lush pastures and smiling skies. When Margaret was born on
her parents' dairy farm there in 1937 she had entered a world that was a
childhood idyll. She was a loved member of a large family with three
brothers and three sisters for company, and while she says that there was
never an abundance of money in the family, all were happy and overflowing
with healthy high spirits.

In those days tractors had not replaced horses for farm work, and the
Greigs' horses were regarded as part of the family — powerful and affectionate animals who, when their share of the work was done, were quite agree-
able to the children scrambling on to their backs. Like her sisters, Margaret
loved riding, and often she saddled up the family pony to ride out over the
farmland and enjoy the unique qualities of the Australian landscape. Its vast-
ness and sense of timelessness is the keynote of the continent which
remained untouched for so long. Away from the cities there is a curious
sense of otherworldness — no doubt the inspiration for the Aborigines'
belief in the Dreamtime — and this atmosphere was stored away in the
young girl's subconscious.

They were good days for the family in the late 1940s. The war was over
and its restrictions had been replaced by a sense of buoyancy, a certainty
that after such a global upheaval nothing like it would be allowed to happen
again — the newly formed United Nations would see to that, while science,
which had taken such strides in devising instruments of destruction, would
now be harnessed for everyone's good.

At Moruya the Greig children learnt about this at school. After lessons
they would carry out their allotted chores and then be free to play and tend
their Fresian calves. This they did with such dedication that they won Junior

Farmer Club prizes for them. Margaret — whose ambition it was to become a nurse — was an enthusiastic member of the club and at field days won several awards for her ability in cattle judging. She also carried off prize ribbons for riding at the local agricultural show.

In 1950 the Press and radio reported a case of poliomyelitis — and a shadow fell over the hearts of parents across the continent. In the days before Salk vaccine epidemics of the disease — originally referred to as Infantile Paralysis — took a grim toll of children in Australia and New Zealand. Schools would be closed, and harassed parents tried to keep their youngsters at home to lessen the risk of infection.

The figures of the victims continued to rise until the spread of the disease became nationwide, but still there was hope that the modern plague would pass by such places as Moruya . . . until one day thirteen-year-old Margaret complained of a raging headache. After the doctor was called he wasted no time. An ambulance whisked her away to hospital, and as it became more and more difficult for her to breathe, it was decided that she would have to go into an iron lung. In normal circumstances the prospect of being shut in the coffin-like apparatus would have been frightening, but Margaret says, 'I was so sick I was past caring. In fact, it was a relief to be in it. Then, as I began to recover, though I was almost completely without movement, it didn't occur to me that I wouldn't be going home and doing the things I had always done. By the time it did, I had already accepted my disability. Perhaps because the Lord was already preparing me for the life He had planned for me, the situation was made easier to accept, and though there were times of sadness and sometimes frustration with the hospital system, there were none of the deep anxieties and rebellion that many suddenly incapacitated people go through. In discussions with other disabled people, many have said the same thing. It doesn't mean there haven't been times of deep sadness and frustration at the inability to get things achieved. That is one reason more that I will be eternally grateful to the Association of Mouth and Foot Painting Artists. Their support has allowed us to become people.'

Margaret was transferred to the Prince Henry Hospital in Sydney where she could receive specialist treatment. Being over two hundred miles away from her home, this change added to the trauma of the illness, because it meant that her parents could not visit her as frequently as they wished. The dairy farm where cows had to be milked twice a day, and Margaret's brothers and sisters, were an endless demand upon them, and on top of that there was the cost of travelling.

It was to be three-and-a-half years before she was able to return to Moruya.

To begin with Margaret was completely paralysed and it was only natural that she should wonder if she would ever have any physical control over her body. Her hopes rose when it was considered that she was well enough to begin an intensive course of physiotherapy. After fifteen months some movement had been regained. Although she did have very limited use of her arms it was obvious that doing ordinary things manually, such as writing, were things of the past and that for the rest of her life she would be confined to a wheelchair.

'If you miss your folks, why don't you try writing home to them?' said a nurse one day when Margaret lay on her stomach, resting from her therapy. She was reading a newspaper and it suddenly occurred to her that if she could read in that position, one could also grip a pen between the teeth and write in it.

Without further ado, the nurse put the end of a ballpoint pen into her mouth and held a pad in front of her face. The result was a collection of wild lines squiggling across the page — they might have put off most people in such a situation, but Margaret was fascinated by them. They represented the very first thing she had done for herself since the day the rubber collar of the iron lung was fitted round her neck.

'It was enough to encourage me to do more each day,' she recalls. 'At first my "writing" was funny, erratic scrawls but gradually it became legible enough for me to write my first letters home. At that time I hadn't heard of other mouth and foot painting artists, but this form of writing led to attempts at drawing, a hobby which I enjoyed at school.'

Not surprisingly, Margaret's early sketches were of horses, drawn from her memories of life on the farm at Moruya. The nursing staff became enthusiastic over her progress and she was given a set of water colours, but though she tried hard to paint with them she was disappointed to find that she could not control them as well as she would have liked.

Her new found ability did have one very important effect on her life, she was able to take a correspondence course while still in hospital, and was thus able to complete her schooling by writing the answers to her lessons with a pen clamped in her teeth. When the course was concluded some friends, anxious that she should keep up a study routine, cast about for another educational activity which would be suitable and came up with the suggestion of a ticket writing course.

Gamely Margaret enrolled for it. She found that there were parts of it which, because of her limited range of movement, she was unable to cope with, but by concentrating on what she was able to do she did manage to complete it. Today she is grateful for the experience because, despite its difficulties, the practice it entailed greatly developed her control of brush and pen.

After three-and-a-half years spent in various hospitals Margaret was allowed to return to her home at Moruya where her family were to look after her with devotion. And what joy it was to be able to sit in her wheel-chair and gaze out over the fields where once — a lifetime ago it seemed — she had galloped her pony.

'I busied myself with many interests, but there was nothing available that would enable me to take up some sort of employment or earn a living for myself,' she says.

After fifteen years Margaret became anxious over her mother's declining health, and she knew that the work involved in looking after her was becoming too much of a burden for her. She knew that she must be the one to make the decision, heartbreaking though it might be, to leave Moruya for a second time. She applied to enter a home for disabled people at Penrith, near Sydney.

The change did not prove to be as bad as she had feared. When a disabled person lives in the world of the physically fit no matter how understanding they may be, there is always some sense of isolation, of being different. Here Margaret found that she was among people whose shared experience of disability created a camaraderie in which the newcomer soon felt at home. Another advantage was that the home had a sheltered workshop attached to it where members of the small community did whatever work their disability allowed them.

'After I had worked in the workshop for quite a while I began doing clerical work in the administrator's office, using a stick held in my mouth to operate the keys of an electric typewriter,' Margaret says. 'It was rather laborious at first but I found it thrilling — it was the first work I had ever done.'

At this time painting, however, remained a hobby. Although Margaret had not had a particularly religious background as a child, she found that her experience of adversity had awakened an interest in spiritual matters which led to a faith which she found gave her strength to cope with her problems. And it was because of her Christian conviction that she agreed to become a Sunday School teacher at a local church when asked.

If she was nervous at first, wondering at the reaction of her class at seeing a lady wheeled before them who could not use her arms or legs, the feeling was soon replaced by one of satisfaction — at least she was not on the receiving end but was able to do something for others. Only those who have suffered incapacity can fully understand the importance of this.

'Becoming a Sunday School teacher opened up a whole wealth of pleasure and involvement which extended into youth groups and becoming aware of the joys, problems and relationships of young people', Margaret explains today. She also became involved in the Christian Fellowship and it was through this that she made friends with Mel Fleming who one day brought

a set of oil paints for her to try. Those paints had belonged to her husband who, after attempting to paint as a hobby, found that he did not enjoy it. Now Mel decided that they might be more suitable for a mouth painter than watercolours which Margaret was never at ease with, and, from the first moment the thick rich colour was transferred from her brush to her canvas, Margaret became excited at the prospect oil paints opened up.

'They were so thrilling to work with that I became engrossed in painting again,' she says. 'A few months later the Association of Mouth and Foot Painting Artists contacted me and that was the real turning point in my life.'

After her work had been evaluated she was accepted as a student member and, being awarded a regular income by the Association while training, she had the greatest satisfaction of writing to the social security authorities to inform them that she no longer needed their support. At last she was independent.

Margaret worked hard to improve her painting and before long her confidence was strengthened by being able to sell some privately, and there was more satisfaction when the Association published her first Christmas card.

As her stock of paintings grew they filled her living area at the hostel until it seemed to be overflowing with canvases. What Margaret really needed was a studio of her own like any other artist. And in 1972 her friend Mel Fleming and her husband came to the rescue. They invited her to move into their home at Londonderry in New South Wales and Mel arranged to have a pleasant studio built for her on a plot of land next door, and it is here that she still works.

At last the time came for Margaret's first exhibition at which she was to demonstrate her method of painting. It was held at Newcastle in NSW and she was relieved that she was to share it with a fellow mouth painter, Bruce Peardon.

'It was real scary at first,' she says. 'Bruce painted away quite happily with people standing round watching him, so I plucked up courage and followed suit. Once I got absorbed in what I was doing I forgot about the spectators.'

Since then Margaret has given demonstrations at exhibitions in many parts of Australia, producing pictures whose themes reflect her early interests and the love she felt for her home landscape as a child. Her paintings feature old farmhouses with their 'colonial' verandahs, walls of time-bleached planks and corrugated-iron roofs now rust coloured — lonely memorials of the pioneering days. Other pictures, often with the bluegums which are so evocative of the Australian landscape, and with the plains of sunburned grass stretching towards distant ranges, convey a feeling of space and timelessness. No doubt the success of Margaret's work is that it evokes an instant recognition for Australians of the spirit of the place.

Horses are still a favourite subject. Sometimes several heavy, woolly-footed draught horses harnessed behind a plough or harrow, as Margaret had seen them when a little girl, are portrayed. Sometimes they appear singly as though turned out to graze after the day's work.

In 1982 Margaret had been so successful as a member of the Association that she was able to build her own home — specially designed to accommodate her wheelchair — on the land behind her studio. She lives there now with a friend, Marie Kelly, a teacher of intellectually handicapped children, and a small family of animals which include three dogs — Belinda, Penny and Smiley — two donkeys, two goats and Prince, a miniature horse whose head is level with the arm rests of her wheelchair.

'I got Prince when he was only four-and-a-half months old,' Margaret says. 'Now he is full grown and just over thirty-one inches high. He is the best company I could have. When I let him come into the studio he stands beside me while I am painting as good as gold. Sometimes he lays his head on my lap and goes to sleep standing up and, like a dog, he is eager to please and loves to be praised.'

Margaret's studio, with its complement of animals, has become a local landmark. It is not unusual for people passing through to stop to chat with Margaret while she works, have a coffee and look at her display of paintings which are for sale. In this way she combines a gallery with her studio and every August holds a special charity exhibition. The proceeds from this go to St George's Association for the Disabled, a society which arranges outings and holiday accommodation for the disabled.

Apart from being able to have her own house and studio after joining the Association, Margaret found that she was able to indulge in what had seemed impossible before, and that was to go touring in a caravanette with her friends Marie Bates and Mel Fleming.

'After I had contracted polio the last thing I thought I would ever be able to do would be to go camping,' Margaret says. 'But I found that to travel in a camper is more convenient than staying at hotels or guest houses. So many are not suited to accommodating disabled people with wheelchairs and this is especially difficult when you are unable to get a room on the ground floor, but you can gear a camper to your needs.'

One of the advantages which Margaret found in making such trips was that it gave her new scenes for her to paint. Although she does not paint outside her studio, she gets her companion to take a huge amount of colour photos of the landscapes she passes through, but what she says is more important is that she is able to 'soak up' the atmosphere of the places which fascinate her. And it is the atmosphere of the Australian countryside which people have found so enjoyable in her paintings.

In the summer of 1985 Margaret decided to have a holiday in England before going to Madrid for a conference to be attended by Mouth and Foot Painters Association members from all over the world. She travelled with her friend Marie Kelly, and another old friend from Londonderry, Marie Bates. And confident that camping was the best way to travel, Margaret and the two Maries hired a caravanette in London in which they made a two-thousand-mile tour which included both the Isle of Wight and the Isle of Skye.

For Margaret the highpoint of her holiday came with a visit to the Kilverstone Wildlife Park in Norfolk which is famous for its miniature horses.

'It fired me with the ambition to get a miniature mare,' she said afterwards. 'It would be so nice for Prince to have a companion of his own size. And then there is the exciting possibility that a foal might be born.'

So life continues for Margaret Greig, surrounded by human friends and her animals in her home set amidst the countryside which she loves to paint. She believes that her disability was meant to be and says, 'I think it is a waste of time to regret what cannot be altered. But just as this physical handicap was intended for me, so was a happy life.'

'I Was Discarded . . .'

ALBERT BAKER

IT had been a very good day for Albert Baker. His paintings were on display in the Queen Elizabeth Hall at London's Royal Festival Hall where he had met His Royal Highness the Duke of Edinburgh who had complimented him on his work. When the reception was over Albert was overtaken by a sudden urge to visit a scene from his past, and he asked a friend who was driving his estate car for him to head for Dartford.

When the vehicle pulled up outside a Victorian building behind high walls memories flooded back to Albert, memories without nostalgia whose only pleasurable aspect was that they reminded him how much his life had changed since he had lived there.

'It used to be called The Spike,' he explains. 'That was the slang name for the workhouse. Now it was no longer used for that purpose. The gates were open and the sentry box, where the inmates were checked in and out, was gone.'

Next Albert was driven to the house in Penge where he had been born in 1922. Here more memories flooded back — memories which were far from happy — before he returned to where he now lived in the lovely Hampshire countryside which was a further reminder of his escape from a life of frustration and dreariness.

Unlike the other artists described in this book, Albert Baker is the only one to have been disabled from birth; his feet were club-footed and he was unable to use his arms or legs. Today he has total recall of his earliest days, being able to remember the faces of his brothers and sisters looking over the edge of his cot and taking him to the park in a pram.

As if it was not bad enough to be born with a disability, he had the added burden of an unhappy home life. His father, who was his mother's second husband, was a man of very short temper and when the little boy cried — with every good reason — he was threatened with the cane which was kept hanging in the coal cellar.

'My father was very cruel to my mother,' Albert says. 'Even in those very early days I sensed how unhappy she was. One of the most horrible things my father ever said was to my half-brother Fred. For some reason he had got angry with the boy, and wanting to hurt him in some way, he pulled the cot covers off me and pointing to my arms and legs, said, "You are the cause of this!"

'Of course the charge was ridiculous, but it was after this incident that Dad kicked him out of the house and he went to live with a neighbour. When Fred was sixteen my father died and Mother asked him to come back but he went away and we never knew what happened to him.

'But that remark of my father's has always remained with me.'

At the age of three Albert went to St Thomas's Hospital for an assessment of his disability, after which he spent some time in the Royal National Orthopaedic Hospital at Stanmore before going to St Nicholas' and St Martin's Orthopaedic Hospital, Now called the Rowley Bristo Hospital — near Purford, Surrey, where he was to remain for the next nine years of his life, from five to fourteen.

A special school was attached to the hospital, but Albert did not get full benefit from it and today he is largely self-taught.

'My schooling was broken up by a number of operations which resulted in my childhood never being free from pain,' he explains. 'At the age of seven

I became interested in painting and drawing. I began fiddling about with a brush held in my mouth — the only way I could manage it. I do not know what sparked off the interest, but I do remember when I was very very young my sister talked about oil colours, artists and how you had to stand well away from oil paintings to appreciate them. This is not necessarily true, but I can always remember her saying that and perhaps it was that which sparked off my fascination with painting.'

In 1936, a week after the death of King George V, Albert was sent to a special craft school by the sea at Seaford in Sussex in the hope of being able to learn a trade but after three months it was decided that he was too handicapped to be taught anything that would help him to earn a living. After leaving school, the boy had to travel by railway which meant that he had to wait for a train at London Bridge station.

'One of the features of St Nicholas' and St Martin's Hospital was an open-air environment, the wards being open to the weather,' says Albert. 'At London Bridge I went into the waiting room where everyone was smoking, and, having spent so much time in the fresh air, it seemed as though a hot, smelly blanket hit me right in the face, suffocating me. It was like going into a gas-filled room. I suppose because smoking had this effect upon me I never took up the habit.' Even today he cannot stand tobacco smoke.

In the same year Albert was sent to a hospital in Dartford where an orthopaedic surgeon examined his legs.

'One day you should be able to walk,' he said, and his words heralded more surgery for the boy.

'I think a lot of my operations were exploratory,' Albert says. 'My mother told me a few months before she died that she signed a paper giving them blanket permission to do whatever they thought necessary, and this allowed them to experiment.

'After an operation on each wrist it left my hands twice as bad as they were before, and from then on I was more dependent on people doing things for me.'

The series of painful operations continued for three years — from 1936 to 1939 — after which he was fitted with special boots and leg irons. These, too, where painful, digging into his flesh as he struggled to step forward. Without the use of his hands to steady himself, Albert often fell over. But gradually, by leaning his body against the wall or pieces of furniture, he was able to cross a room on his own, and from this he finally managed to walk — or waddle, as he says.

This period of treatment ended when he was seventeen. His mother was asked if she would have him at home, but this was not possible because of her strained circumstances which made it necessary for her to live on public assistance which provided her with ten shillings a week and in those days there was no financial assistance for the disabled.

'I was discarded,' Albert declares. 'The only place for me to go was the workhouse which was run under the Poor Law system which was then still in operation.'

His mother fought bravely against this, pleading with the authorities not to put her son away amongst a lot of geriatric men. As a result of her efforts he was allowed in the hospital wing of the workhouse for the next three years.

'I had a miserable time in there,' he says. 'During my stay I only went out once. That was to a Dr Barnado's boys concert in the Dartford Town Hall.'

One of the things which he found upsetting was that he was mocked because of his disability.

'I could manage to waddle along in those days,' he recalls. 'The others used to make fun of me over that, calling me Albert Ramsbottom, not because of Stanley Holloway's monologue about Albert and the Lion, but because my backside stuck out when I walked. It was started by a member of the staff who should have known better. Letters were even addressed to me by that name.

'People can be very cruel and being very sensitive made it worse for me. That is why I tend to get bitter when I'm upset. It is something within me which built up over the years, but even the worm will turn, and I don't stand any nonsense these days.'

In 1939 Albert was transferred to a hospital 'for incurables and cripples' which was run by monks in Yorkshire.

'As far as I was concerned it was a glorified workhouse,' says Albert. 'Of course I was happy to be in the country and the best thing about being there was that I was able to go out for walks. At that time I was able to manage a mile, though over the years I have lost the ability. The place was run under a very strict regime. Once, when I was in the nearby village, one of the monks saw me speak to a woman there — in actual fact I was just passing the time of day! — and when I got back to the hospital I was told that if I was caught doing it again I should be sent away.'

Albert was to stay in the hospital for incurables and cripples for fourteen years, during which he painted postcards in watercolour as a hobby by holding a brush in his mouth as he had done when a child.

He was greatly inspired by the beauty of the landscape through which he went for his painful walks and he would have given anything to be able to do 'real' pictures, but the hospital was understaffed and there was no one to help him. So he stuck to his postcards, producing several a week which he sold for a shilling each. A disheartening aspect of this occupation was that sometimes he found water had been tipped over his work as a joke.

Towards the end of his stay at the home conditions deteriorated alarmingly. It reached a situation in which there were not enough attendants to help patients who had some mobility to get up, with the result that some disabled residents, who had been able to go for walks, now had to spend twenty-four hours a day in bed.

To Albert the hospital had become yet another nightmare, and he wrote anxious letters to his mother to see if she could look after him. She agreed and it was without regrets that Albert left Yorkshire and returned to London where he became an outpatient at King's College Hospital in Denmark Hill. Here, thanks to occupational therapy, life began to improve at last. He managed to do more for himself, including shaving by rubbing his cheek against a fixed razor, and he continued to sell postcards which he painted, though he received very little from this as it took him a whole day to produce one. And although Albert's only real pleasure was derived from his art work, the depressing thing was that the earnings from the only possible thing he could do were not worthwhile. He was dependent on his mother and, only too aware of her past struggle against poverty, he yearned to support himself above everything else.

Nearly three years after he had left Yorkshire, it became clear that, because of her age, his mother found it a struggle to look after him, and it was arranged that he should be admitted to the Le Court Leonard Cheshire Foundation in Hampshire. This was the first of the famous homes founded by Group Captain Leonard Cheshire, who conceived the idea of founding homes to be places of shelter and of spiritual encouragement when he took an ex-serviceman, who was dying of cancer, into his own home. Today there are many Cheshire Homes in this country and abroad, and any person who is physically disabled, regardless of race or creed, can apply to become a resident.

To Albert, Le Court meant the beginning of a new life when he arrived there in March, 1956. The aim of the Cheshire Homes is to be as 'un-institutional' as possible, and here in a garden setting and surrounded by beautiful trees and banks of rhododendrons, Albert found a contentment which he had never before known. His only regret was that he could not pay his way.

It was at this pint that Erich Stegmann, the founder of the Association of Mouth and Foot Painting Artists, came upon the scene. He had heard of a man who painted postcards by mouth in England, and he was eager to contact him.

'The Association had been trying to get in touch with me for a long time but they did not know where I lived,' says Albert. 'When they did discover my whereabouts they came and saw my paintings. I was then offered a studentship and this meant that I could undertake a course of art lessons at

93

Le Court with a teacher named Barbara Waller. She taught me all the good habits and how to unlearn the bad ones which were a result of being self taught.'

Under tuition the standard of Albert's painting steadily improved, helped also by the fact that for the first time he could afford professional art materials. After four years of very hard work his paintings were assessed by an independent panel which judged it to be of the same quality one would expect from an able-bodied artist who sold work professionally. He became a full member of the Association and has always felt a deep sense of gratitude to Erich Stegmann who had been so eager to locate him.

Speaking about him today he says, 'Stegmann used his genius for the good of others. What more charitable act can you do than to restore a man's faith and confidence in himself, or give it to him if he has lacked it before? In the past I felt so useless that I thought of doing away with myself but he gave me self-respect which I had never known before.'

Being a full member not only meant that from then on Albert would be self sufficient financially but it opened all sorts of doors which earlier would have seemed as impossible as Cinderella's dream of going to the ball. For the first time he was able to travel. At regular intervals Delegates' Conferences are held in different countries by the Mouth and Foot Painting Artists, and in attending Albert has been as far afield as Spain, Austria, Switzerland and India, while among the places he has holidayed are France and the United States where one of the most memorable moments was a visit to the White House.

Thanks to an invalid car provided by the Ministry of Health, Albert has scoured the surrounding countryside in search of views to paint. The vehicle is steered by a tiller arrangement which responds to the movement of his body. The ignition and other controls have been adapted to respond to a mouth stick. To go to more distant places Albert saved up and bought an estate car, and later an ambulance which is fitted with an electric hoist at the rear which takes all the difficulty out of getting aboard in a wheelchair.

Thanks to these vehicles Albert has been able to attend the Association's art exhibitions where he has met fellow disabled artists and given demonstrations of the mouth painting technique which always delight press photographers.

The most exciting exhibition he took part in was one in The Queen Elizabeth Hall where he demonstrated his skill to the Duke of Edinburgh.

'When I was there I remembered how, when I was in the home in Yorkshire, I had seen pictures of the wedding of Princess Elizabeth and the Duke: then the last thing that I could have ever imagined was that someday I should actually meet Prince Philip,' Albert says. 'It was an extraordinary day as it was afterwards that I visited the old workhouse where I had spent three years. It brought home a great deal to me. There I was, having been congratulated on my paintings by a member of royalty, in my own car and with plenty of money in my pocket, yet when I left that place everything I had in the world was in one small case and I did not even have any proper clothes . . .

'Memories of my mother and what she had had to put up with came back to me very strongly. Poor woman, she never had anything and, although I am disabled, I have earned more money since I started painting professionally than she ever saw in her whole life. Had she still been alive I would have been able to share a home with her, and it would have been my turn to look after her . . .'

Albert is living proof of the axiom that the busier you are, the busier you get. At Le Court he continues to paint four or five pictures a month. At weekends local children visit him to clean his brushes and set out canvases for the following week. And because of his interest in young people he was particularly gratified when, in 1984, he was appointed as one of the governors of the Church of England primary school at Greatham. He takes this role very seriously and has helped the school to obtain a computer, as well as a couple of microscopes and beehives which have been set in the school's nature reserve.

Recently Albert was being driven through a storm along the lanes from

Le Court to the school where a fund raising fair was being held when a tree crashed across the road only thirty feet ahead of the vehicle. Undeterred, Albert asked the driver to make a long detour so that he eventually arrived with his picture which was auctioned for the school's benefit and fetched fifty-seven pounds. Only afterwards did Albert realize how close he had been to a terrible accident.

This enthusiasm for young people and the school is a reflection on the character of Albert Baker when one remembers the misery of his own school days. He has come a long way since it was considered funny to spill water on his paintings.

'I had to fight for it'

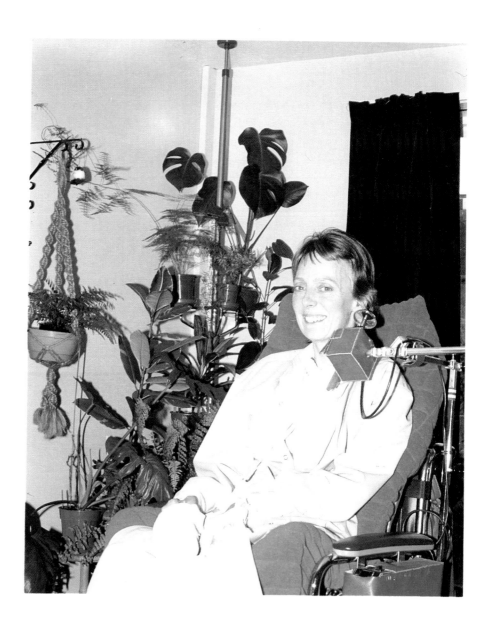

JOY CLARKE

JOY Clarke is a born painter. She had been painting with a mouth-held brush for only three months when samples of her work were sent to the Mouth and Foot Painting Artists' Association — with the result that she was invited to become a student. Just over two years later, in September, 1985, she was made a full member. To have achieved this so quickly suggests that her natural talent for small and exquisite flower and animal studies made it easy for her. This is far from the case — very little in life has been easy for Joy.

There were occasions during the six years when she was shunted from hospital to hospital with a worsening physical condition when she admits that she was so depressed she wanted to die: 'I saw nothing in life, and I was no use to my children.'

This feeling reached a climax when it was suggested that a place might be found for her in a home which catered for the chronically sick. She was taken to see it and here came the realization that she could not face the rest of her days in an institution.

'The place was full of tragic folk who appeared to be twice my age gazing blankly into space,' Joy says. 'It decided me that if I was going to do anything with my life I had to fight for it.'

Because of the nature of her complaint, Joy is one of those disabled people who do not fit into a recognised category. Consequently the authorities found it a problem as to what to do with her. She finally solved the problem by living on her own!

Before she achieved this — thanks to her determination and unsuspected talent as an artist — Joy had to suffer many years in the wilderness. Her life has had more than its fair share of problems, starting with her childhood in Parkestone, Dorset, where her mother was a victim of a rare neurological disease known as the Charcot-Marie Tooth Syndrome.

'Despite my mother's illness and money problems, I loved Dorset and had a good childhood,' Joy recalls. 'I first realized that there was something not quite right with me when I was sixteen. I was still at school and I found that I could not do things in the gym that once came easily to me. I had the usual school medical and was sent to be seen by an orthopaedic surgeon because my feet had become an awful shape and were very painful. At the time it did not enter my head that my mother's condition could be hereditary, even though her trouble had begun with her feet.

'My mother had suffered so much that I think she could not accept that there was anything really wrong with me. She wanted to ignore it, and I think she was quite firm, if not rude, to the surgeon who wanted to do something about my feet and the whole matter was dropped.'

Joy soon had other things to think about. Because her mother was ill and without a husband, she decided that although she had started an A-level course, she would have to leave school and get work to keep the home going. She went in for horticulture which was to prove of immense value to her many years later in a way which she could not have guessed at.

For a year Joy worked at a garden nursery during the day and spent every moment of her free time looking after her mother, which became more and more difficult as her illness progressed.

'A time came when I could no longer cope with earning enough to keep the home going and looking after her, especially as her illness had affected her mentally,' Joy says. The result was that it was arranged for her mother to live in a Cheshire Home in Hampshire, and Joy and her brother went to live with relatives in Rugby where she continued the horticultural work which she loved.

'In those days we worked a statutory forty-seven hours a week, and often we put in eighty,' Joy explains. 'There was no overtime agreement but from time to time we would get a bonus from the boss. People would not work like that today, but I enjoyed it and tried to ignore the fact that my feet were becoming more misshapen. I spent my days in Wellington boots and I changed into slippers when I got home. The truth was that I could no longer wear ordinary shoes.'

Joy sought medical advice, and was taken into hospital for an operation on her feet which at first seemed successful. At this time she still felt confident about her future and, at the age of twenty-one, she got married. Sadly the benefit derived from the operation did not last. Joy was subjected to specialized medical investigation, with the result that the same disease which afflicted her mother was diagnosed. Added to this was the complication of a circulatory problem.

Although as time went on and Joy's physical difficulties imperceptibly increased, she did manage to lead a normal life and at the age of twenty-seven gave birth to her daughter, her son being born the following year. The happiness of having a young family was marred by marital tensions, and two years later she was forced to get a divorce.

For the next three years Joy continued to look after her children alone, but her growing disability made this more and more difficult as by now she had to use crutches to move about the house.

'It was terrible when the children were little and I had to send them up to bed alone,' says Joy. 'I just could not get upstairs to tuck them in and kiss them goodnight. And there were all sorts of little difficulties which were making life increasingly awkward. For example, I seemed to be losing strength and sensation in my hands and I could not fit the key in the lock when I came home. The children were not tall enough to do it for me, so I would have to send them to a neighbour's for help. Even the fact that I could not take the lids off jars or unscrew bottle caps added to my domestic problems.'

Another thing which worried Joy at that time was the attitude of her local church. She had always been a practising Christian but when she went to services in a trouser suit, which she wore to hide the condition of her feet and legs, she was told 'it was not the done thing', nor was supporting herself by means of her child's push-chair — before she had crutches.

As a result a friend introduced her to the United Reformed Church whose congregation was more understanding, and of which she has been a member ever since. She is adamant that her faith was her greatest support through the dark times which lay ahead.

These dark times commenced in 1977 when, to use Joy's words, 'things started to rocket'.

'I was very worried and anxious and had realized things were probably seriously wrong before I went into hospital,' she says. 'I found that in running a home there was more and more that I was unable to cope with, just as years earlier I knew that I had lost my agility when I was in the gym.'

The combination of her neurological disorder and her circulatory complaint made her so ill that in hospital she had to face the fact that she would no longer be able to look after her children, and with all the courage she could summon up she set about the heart-breaking task of arranging for them to be fostered..Then in September, 1978, it was found necessary to amputate her leg. Eighteen months later she lost her other leg and on top of this she discovered that she was losing the use of her hands and arms.

Joy spent two years in the first hospital and when it seemed that nothing more could be done for her there she was moved from place to place. A couple of years were spent in the ward of a geriatric hospital.

'The state of the ward was something you read about but which you cannot believe happens,' she says. Although the staff were kind to her — and in a wheelchair she was able to offer conversation to some of her fellow inmates who otherwise would have sat in silence — it was not a suitable place for a young woman. This period came to an end when she had to go to an orthopaedic hospital in Coventry for an operation. When the surgeon learned that she would be returning to a geriatric ward, he arranged for her to be kept in his hospital.

This suited Joy much better, but when the Health Authority was reorganized it was decreed that she could no longer stay there because she was out of her official area, so once more she was without a permanent place.

'While the authorities were trying to decide what to do with me it was suggested I be put in a home for incurables, and I fought like mad against that,' Joy recalls. Finally she ended up in the corner of a cardiac medical ward. Here the problem was that she was the odd one out.

'I was miserable for weeks,' she says. 'Understandably the staff were too busy to bother with me when they literally had to save people's lives. Sometimes I lay in bed half the day, waiting for a wash or a drink. The worst thing was that I reached a point where I was unable to turn the pages of a book or newspaper, so even reading was denied to me.'

It was during such periods that Joy found there was an irritable side to her nature.

'I did get very irate over things,' she admits. 'Until then I had been a placid person but I began to get irritable, cross and tearful — everything! And I still do on occasions. I think it is all to do with frustration, and with the authorities trying to organize me and my future, I felt I was just an object. It gave me that bit of fight but, to be quite honest, I must have been abominable.'

But that 'bit of fight' was just what Joy needed.

'I remember, before completely losing the use of my right hand, I decided that I would learn to write holding a pen in my mouth because I thought I'd be blowed if I would be in the position where I could not sign my own cheques. It was difficult because I could not sit up properly then but I propped paper on a pillow beside me and tried to scribble. Knowing what lay in store for me, the nursing officer gave me encouragement.

'I also decided that I could not spend the rest of my life lying in bed, and, having heard about the Mary Marlborough Lodge — a residential unit attached to the famous Nuffield Orthopaedic Hospital just outside Oxford which served the British Isles as an artificial limb and appliance centre — I mentioned this to my surgeon. I thought that my first step was to get a wheelchair that I would be able to sit in because I found that I just fell out of ordinary ones.

'It was agreed that I should go there and, although it had been my idea, I found I was terrified of going. I hate change and having people I do not know doing things for me. But when I got there I found it was fantastic and forgot all my doubts.'

The famous rehabilitation centre provided Joy with a wheelchair which she could control by the small amount of movement left in her hand. Three months later she lost this facility and found herself back in bed for another year.

It was one day in 1982, when Joy was in the Hospital of St Cross in Rugby, that the registrar, worried by the danger of becoming trapped in a vegetable-like existence, suggested that she should set about doing something such as writing . . . or painting. Now completely without the use of her arms, and unable to sit up properly, his suggestion might have seemed impossible but Joy seized upon it.

'I spoke about it to the occupational therapist who said if I could get strapped into a wheelchair safely for an hour I could have a go. I was determined to try. Rather unsuitable paper was pinned to a piece of hardboard which was propped up on books and, half-lying in an awkward position, a brush was put in my mouth.

'Using a child's box of watercolour paints I set to work as best I could, and the first thing that I did was a Christmas card with a candle and a piece of holly round the bottom. Although I say it myself it was good — had it

been awful I would never have tried again.'

It was then mid-October and Joy decided that she would paint all her Christmas cards. At first she could only manage to sit up for an hour, but she was so keen to extend her painting sessions that she forced herself to stay up longer and longer. The result was that by Christmas she had painted twenty-six cards, a few of which she kept because she could not bear parting with them. This was to be an unexpected stroke of luck.

After Christmas Joy's therapist said, 'Have you ever thought about the Mouth and Foot Painting Artists?'

Joy knew about them because her mother had used their cards, but the thought of approaching the organization had never occurred to her. The therapist told her that she would write for details.

'I thought it was ludicrous,' Joy declares. 'I had only been painting three months and could not do anything very large because — unlike a lot of mouth-painters — I could not control long-handled brushes, and due to the nature of my disability I do not have the reach for wide pictures.'

Back came the reply: the Association was just as interested in small pictures as in any others and suggested that Joy send in ten samples of her work. Joy blessed the fact that she had held back some of her Christmas cards and sent them off.

Until May she was on tenterhooks. It seemed impossible that after painting for such a short time the Association could be impressed by her work — on the other hand, if they were, what a difference it would make to her life! It would give her something definite to aim for. Then came a letter informing her that as from the first of June she would receive a student's stipend.

This meant that at last she was able to get proper equipment and artists' materials, and it was arranged for a retired artist to visit her regularly to give her the benefit of his advice.

'At this point he was very helpful, especially when it came to advising me on skies and backgrounds,' Joy says, 'but I think the best way to learn is to make your own mistakes.' These backgrounds became the settings for beautifully detailed flower arrangements which, with her knowledge of plants gained in the days when she worked in horticulture, are her favourite subjects.

Delicacy is their hallmark, and the fact that it is appreciated was borne out when Joy held her first exhibition. It was held in an art gallery attached to a Rugby garden centre where she had worked many years ago, and of the thirty-three paintings which were hung, twenty-four were sold, an amazing compliment for a new artist.

'Joining the Association was a turning point for me,' Joy says. 'Apart from anything else it enabled me to save up to buy my present electric wheelchair, the seat of which was made for me at the Mary Marlborough Lodge in Oxford which enabled me to sit up for long periods — which gradually became all day — in relative comfort and in an orthopaedically correct position.'

With her new interest in painting Joy felt that she had a new lease of life, and other possibilities entered her mind which until then had seemed to be impossible dreams. Above all she wanted to get away from institutional life and have her home again. She knew that, thanks to the Mouth and Foot Painters' Association, others had been able to regain their independence, and perhaps when she became a full member the same might be possible for her.

As it happened the dream became a reality sooner than she expected.

It began when a relative and her husband visited Joy in the St Cross Hospital where they were duly impressed by her painting. As a result — and without Joy knowing anything about it — the couple contacted the Social Services to see, if they came and lived with her, she could be provided with somewhere to live. The Social Services agreed and the idea was presented to Joy as a *fait accompli* which came as a great surprise to her. On one hand it would mean that she would be in the outside world after five-and-a-half years of institutional life; on the other hand she had doubts as to whether she would find life compatible with her relatives.

She discussed the pros and cons with a social worker who suggested that she give it a six-month trial, after which it could be decided whether the arrangement was satisfactory from everyone's point of view as well as from the medical aspect.

Although she had private misgivings, Joy made up her mind that she would try anything to begin a new life. It was decided that to begin with she should only spend two-and-a-half days a week away from the hospital until it was established that it would be medically safe for her to return full time to the outside world. The Social Services found her a bungalow, situated in the grounds of an old people's home, which had once been used by the caretaker but which had stood empty for a number of years. Despite its air of neglect, the thing which immediately found favour with Joy was its garden, despite the fact that it was waist-high with weeds.

Joy's relatives moved in and she joined them, and from the start she felt reassured that it was for a six months' trial because of her doubts as to how they would get on together. Therefore it came as a shock when she learned by accident that by the third week her relatives had sold their house in the south of England — obviously the idea of a trial period had been ignored. Once more Joy felt that she was being treated as an object, that her future was being planned without her being consulted. At the same time she had to return to hospital for an operation, and the consultant, who was deeply aware of the problem, advised her to write to her relatives telling them that, as far as she was concerned, the arrangement was not working out.

'It was the worst thing I ever had to do, but I did it then and there,' said Joy. 'I knew that if I thought about it for the rest of the day I should not have the courage to do it.' The consultant later asked Joy if she would be prepared to live on her own.

'Of course I could!' Joy replied, determined to do it at all costs. But she had to spend another year in hospital until a system of help could be worked out, during which time she continued to pay the rent and rates on the bungalow so she should not lose it.

Today Joy lives alone in her bungalow which she has transformed into a tastefully furnished home in which a surprising number of houseplants thrive. When she took it over there was no furniture or carpets, but a grant from the Mouth and Foot Artists' Association went a long way to bringing it to its present state.

In her special electric wheelchair which she bought for herself, Joy is able to move deftly about her livingroom, and travel from room to room by means of a simple control which is activated by pressure from the chin. To begin with, the control box was mounted in front of her and got in the way of painting, so Joy devised a method by which she could slide it to one side when necessary. Because the company which fitted it realized that this innovation could be used for disabled people with similar problems to Joy's, they were happy to convert her wheelchair free of charge.

'Shortly after being issued with this chin-controlled chair — and when I had tasted the freedom self-mobility offered — the realization of the limitations of having a Ministry loaned (if you like) electric chair dawned on me,' says Joy. 'These chairs, with proportional controls, are specially "doctored" for the Ministry, with blocks on the motors to slow them down from an already walking pace speed of approximately 4 mph to a deathly 1 mph. This is adequate for safe travel inside a small home but hopeless, in fact deliberately made impossible, for outdoor mobility. Their power and wheels are such that they cannot cope with rough terrain, lawns and even slight gradients. The distance travelled round the home is about all that can be managed, hence the ruling that they should not be used beyond the confines of one's home. No self-driven, electrically or otherwise powered chair for outdoor use can be supplied by the Ministry. This fact, coupled with my longing for more freedom and independence, started the search and the saving up for my present private powered chair, which had to be suitably designed to accommodate my special seat, without which my very existence in my home, and my career as an artist, could not have been accomplished.'

J.C.

105

Although she is alone both day and night, Joy obviously needs help in getting up, going to bed and in the preparation of meals. Three mornings a week a helper comes in from the Crossroads scheme, and every morning nurses arrive to get her up and dress her; in the evening she has similar help in going to bed. Home helps are provided for the domestic work but Joy still encounters the frustrations with which many disabled people can sympathize. Sometimes they are little things such as not being able to pick up a vase of flowers that has fallen over, but which are vivid reminders of one's predicament.

But if life on her own does have some drawbacks, the compensations are overwhelming. First and foremost is her pleasure in her garden which she created from a wilderness. Although she obviously cannot actually tend it, and has employed someone to do the physical work, she has had the satisfaction of planning it and buying the plants — many of them evergreen conifers and heathers — and, thanks to her electric wheelchair, she is able to enjoy her old love for growing things.

Often, when her son and daughter pay their regular visit on Friday evenings, they put in new plants or do some weeding.

'Their foster mother Sylvia has been marvellous with them, and luckily they have been with her all along,' Joy says. 'Inevitably they have become more like her children than mine, but that is another of those things which you have to accept. I am grateful that I have a good relationship with them, and now they are older — my daughter is fourteen — I am able to talk to them about my situation in a way which I could not when they were younger. I have been able to explain at least that when I arranged to have them fostered it was not because I did not want to have to look after them any more, but because I believed it was the very best thing for them . . . an act of love.'

Each day Joy steers herself into a spare room which has become her studio, and where she has a special easel which allows her to park with her wheelchair partly beneath it so that her head is close to the curved board — curved to give her more 'reach' with her short-handled brushes — on which her special paper is pinned. Beside it is a small box of watercolours, a water pot and directly below a rack of brushes angled so that it is easy for her to clasp the specially moulded handles with her teeth.

She particularly likes to paint flowers, saying, 'You have to have a love for the things you paint.'

Because she is not as fast as able-bodied artists, she had problems in painting actual flowers. During the day they would change colour and buds would burst into flower so now she has the arrangement photographed so that she can work on it at leisure.

Life is still not easy for Joy. Each day she has to have painkilling drugs and at the time of writing this chapter she is faced with another major operation. Yet, despite her setbacks, she has the satisfaction of being independent and supporting herself by painting the things she loves.

107

'Everyone has a Star ...'

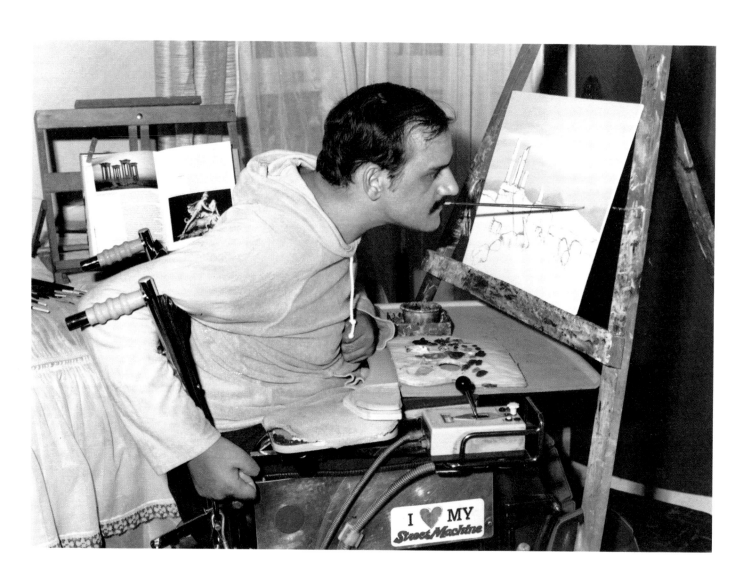

KRIS KIRK

AT five o'clock on Saturday mornings fifteen-year-old Kris Kirk would leave his home in Peckham so as to be in Southall to play Rugby with the Christopher Wren School's First XV by ten. To him this extra early rising was no chore even though on weekdays he had to leave home at six to be on time at the school which was situated in Shepherd's Bush. He loved the sport-oriented school, and he loved being captain of the First XV.

At that time — in 1973 — his achievements on the junior sportsfield were remarkable. Not only was he captain of the school rugby team, but also captained its cricket and baseball teams. As a rugby player he had represented Lonon, Middlesex and South East England — so far his only disappointment had been not getting selected to play for England. But at the end of the trial match he consoled himself by saying, 'I'm only one game away from making it to the England team — next year I will make it.'

The weekend following the trial Kris went on a family outing to Brighton. Although he was born in England, both his parents came from Cyprus and retained the Greek Cypriot sense of 'family', and such outings provided members of the family with an opportunity to get together.

That day Kris and his cousin raced each other over the beach and into the sea. They saw that people were diving off a groyne and joined them. Kris made several successful dives but in his last one his head struck the bottom.

'When I came up to the surface I opened by eyes and found that I could not move,' Kris recalls today. 'My body refused to obey me and I just floated. My cousin thought I was messing about the way kids do, but then he must have realized that something was wrong because he dived in after me and pulled me out of the sea. On the beach the family gathered round me but I still could not move. Then an ambulance came and rushed me to Brighton Hospital.

Here it was discovered that the boy had broken his neck. He was put into traction for two days and then taken to Stoke Mandeville Hospital which is famous for its treatment of spinal cases.

'It wasn't too bad, really,' says Kris. 'I mean it wasn't good, but I was surprised to find that I was still alive. In those days I had thought that breaking your neck automatically meant death.'

Twelve years later Kris Kirk is a handsome young man whose broad shoulders still suggest an athlete — he was an enthusiastic body-builder before his accident — and apart from the fact that he sits in a wheelchair, it is hard to imagine that he is disabled — until one realizes that apart from a little movement in his arms he has no power to control the movement of his hands or body.

With the same determination which almost got him into the England junior rugby team, he leads as normal a life as possible, and this is reflected in his room in the house which he shares with his parents and brother and sister. One wall is lined with reference archaeology and history books — especially books on Ancient Greece and Cyprus — a treasured collection of video tapes and a computer which he daily challenges to chess and more esoteric games. In one corner stands a sleek astronomical telescope; in a cabinet is a collection of pottery brought back from Cyprus and an ikon with a beautiful rizer which was worked by a disabled friend he met at Stoke Mandeville, while on the walls and shelves are the paintings which have made his independent way of life possible.

At Stoke Mandeville, where Kris was treated for a year, physiotherapists did their best to revive his muscular control. When it became clear that he could never regain the use of his hands, various devices were fitted to them in the hope that he could write by utilizing what movement he had left in his arm. Unfortunately — or perhaps fortunately as things have turned out — there were too many drawbacks. The gadgetry was too complicated and Kris would always be reliant on someone being able to fit him up when he needed it. Then it was decided that it would be much simpler if he could learn to write holding a pencil in his teeth, and to this end he began practising in the occupational therapy department.

'They thought it would be useful if I could write my name and even write letters,' Kris explains. 'At that time, even though I had taken an O-level in art, it did not occur to me that there was any future for me as an artist. But when I was not busy practising my letters, I did try a drawing. It was of a lion, but as to how good it was I can only say that when my doctor came on his rounds and saw it he quoted, "Tyger, Tyger burning bright ..."'

When Kris returned home his studies continued. Because it was impossible for him to attend school teachers came to his home to set his lessons and help him with the work. One of the visiting teachers specialized in art and when it was seen that he was able to make progress with a mouth-held pencil, it was arranged for him to go to college one day a week where his art lessons were furthered to the point where he got an A-level. Then a Government-backed organization named Rehab arranged for an art teacher to visit him.

At this time Kris did not find the work very stimulating: 'I was doing drawing but sometimes it would take me weeks to draw a potato on a plate or something like that.'

A step forward was when one of his teachers took him on to the use of poster paints, but it was his final Rehab teacher, an artist named Fred Bloomfield, who had an impact upon him which was to shape his future life.

Today Kris is as enthusiastic as ever about the art teacher who became his friend and mentor.

'He's an incredible artist,' he says. 'He likes to paint surreal subjects best, and sometimes he'll work on a canvas for a year until it's perfect. When you see his pictures you feel you can take the subjects out of the frame, they seem so real.

'He was — and still is — a real friend. He gave me loads of technical advice, and even suggested that someday I might make a living out of painting. Then my time with Rehab ran out but Fred still visits me from time to time, to look at my work and offer advice, and to show me his own.'

Now that his studies were officially over, Kris felt the need to get regular employment and went after various jobs which, while they had nothing to do with art, might be suitable for a disabled person. In every case he was accepted but to his deep disappointment he found that the difficulties in getting to and from the place of work were too great, as in those days he did not have his own means of transport.

'I realised sadly that I could only work from home,' he says, 'but there was not much opportunity for that. Then in 1978 I remembered that a physiotherapist had once told me about an organization for disabled artists, people who were unable to paint with their hands and instead did it by mouth or foot. At the time I had let it go by — somehow it did not occur to me that I might be suitable — but now I got in touch with them.'

The artist Charles Fowler, whose story is told elsewhere in this book, visited Kris on behalf of the Mouth and Foot Painters Association.

'He looked through all my work and chose four to take away for the association to assess,' Kris says. 'At Christmas I received word from the association, and it was the best Christmas present I have ever had. The MFPA was willing to take me on as a student which meant that I would be helped financially, art materials would be provided and if necessary a teacher would be employed to help me improve my standard. And for me the great thing was that I would be able to work from home.

'At that time nearly all of my work was surrealistic because of the influence of my teacher Fred Bloomfield. Now I realized would have to widen my scope — after all you can't have surreal calender and Christmas card pictures — and I also knew that I had a lot of work to do before I could qualify for full membership of the association. The fact that you are disabled is not taken into account when your work goes before the panel of judges. Their criteria is that it is up to the standard of normal professional artists no matter how it is produced.'

Now the most important thing in Kris' life was to be accepted by the MFPA. Each day by ten o'clock he had been got up, dressed and had been given his breakfast, and was ready for the day's work with a brush clamped in his teeth. He would work solidly, with only a half hour break, until about seven o'clock in the evening when he would be too exhausted to continue.

Every three months Kris would submit at least sixteen of his best paintings done during that period which was an extraordinary output for someone doing mouth painting. In 1982 his efforts were rewarded when he was made a full member of the association.

'That was the best thing that ever happened to me since my accident,' he says. 'It has certainly brought me most of what I wanted. And I have found the MFPA to be completely understanding. For example, I am troubled with recurring kidney infection as a result of being incapacitated, and when this happens it is impossible for me to paint, yet I am not made to feel that I am letting them down — one could take months off if necessary and they would understand. I reckon that out of the year I spend an average of three months with medical problems, and there are not many jobs that you could hold down under such circumstances.

'I am not told how many paintings I have to produce, nor has anyone said to me, "I need this type of work or that type of work."'

One of the positive results of becoming an MFPA member was that the following year Kris could afford to turn a long-held dream into reality — he visited Cyprus, the island of his forefathers. With his mother and father, sister and brother, he travelled overland to Greece and thence to Cyprus via Crete which was a bold adventure for someone who had been confined to his home for so long.

'I did not go by airline because I thought that if I had my own transport once we got there we could travel about the island — at least the Greek part of the island,' he explains. 'The bad part of the journey was before we actually set off — there was so much to think of. My special mattresses had to be taken with us as well as a lot of medical equipment. But once we were on our way driving across Europe I felt fine. Rather than have the problems which might arise with me staying at strange hotels, we camped out which added to the fun. We spent nights in Belgium, Germany, Yugoslavia and Greece. Then we had a two day voyage to Cyprus where we stayed for six weeks.

'The best of all was when we reached the island. It was the first time I had ever visited the place where my Mum and Dad came from. All my mother's family are in England, but all my father's family are over there. It was the first time I had met any of them. It was great . . . it was upsetting . . . it was everything you could want. It was an experience of a lifetime.'

Kris was overwhelmed by new sensations, by the heat and colour of the island, by its beaches and ancient buildings and above all by the warmth of the welcome given to him by his relatives who all live in a small refugee village having had to flee their homes at the time of the Turkish invasion.

'In England I had spent a lot of time watching television,' Kris says, 'but during the six weeks I was in Cyprus I can't remember watching a single programme because there was always so much to do. All my Dad's relations now live within a mile of each other and they are always at each other's houses, or going to the beach together, and every day they play backgammon out of doors just as they eat out of doors. At first I thought all this was because we were on holiday, but as time went by I realized that this was

their ordinary way of life. For me it was like paradise, and the only shadow was the political situation.

'From the village we could see Famagusta where my mother and father grew up and which is in Turkish possession now. There's no fence to stop you walking to it, but you just know you can't go. According to the locals if you dared to go there it'd probably be the last time you were seen.

'My Dad's family lost everything they had worked for almost overnight . . . houses, cars, clothes, jewellery, everything yet compared to many they were lucky because they got away without anybody being killed.'

In travelling about the Greek part of Cyprus, Kris was inspired by the scenery and the monuments, and above all by the sense of history which pervades the place and which has made him an avid student of Cyprus' past ever since.

He tried painting out of doors but the heat defeated him. But when he visisted one monastery he found a number of monks painting ikons out of doors in their heavy black robes. Apart from wondering how they stood up to the heat, Kris was fascinated to watch them at work although he did not stay with them as long as he would have liked. The reason for this was that on a slope below the monastery the monks had their beehives and, according to Kris, 'great big monstrous bees buzzed round and frightened the living daylights out of me.' His words summon up a comical picture, until one remembers that people like Kris cannot brush insects away.

Apart from his visit to Cyprus and everything that it meant to him, Kris has found that life has changed in other ways since he joined the partnership of disabled artists. At the time this book was being written he had just taken delivery of a highly sophisticated wheelchair from Germany which, costing around three thousand pounds, would have been far beyond his reach in his pre-MFPA days.

'Because I am lucky enough to have a job with the association I can get extras which the state does not provide,' he says. 'And I know what it's like to have an electric wheelchair provided by the health services. If you dare to go outside in one and go off a kerb I guarantee you'll fall over. It just isn't built for that kind of thing. You need something like this to go out — it gives you a range of thirty miles which is twice that of those little plastic electric vehicles which have come on to the market. It'll go up and down off kerbs with no worry, it's got an electronic braking system so there's no problem if you are in trouble and an electric reclining back so that if you get tired you can lie back. It's a shame that you have to pay to get something like this which you really need if you want to be at all mobile.

'If you are disabled like me you have to make money to get what you really need, and this is where I have been so lucky with the MFPA. In fact, if I had not been working for them I could never have gone to Cyprus. You get a state mobility allowance of course but it will not buy you your own vehicle such as the van I now have, and if you are looking for one with a lift at the back to get your wheelchair aboard you are talking about a lot of money.

'The MFPA is more than a job — it's like a social service. I mean, ordinary people do not worry how they are going to walk to work or maybe visit a beach, whereas if you haven't got a van and if you haven't got a wheelchair that's going to move you about when you get there, you have to stay at home all the time.

Perhaps the greatest pleasure which Kris' super-wheelchair has brought him is being able to leave his home to 'walk' his dog a friendly Doberman Pinscher who responds enthusiastically to the name of Czar, in a nearby park. Like many other disabled people Kris has developed an affinity with his pet which has helped him greatly when life has been difficult.

Czar came to Kris as a pup on his return from Cyprus, and before him he had a Collie named Lad who had been his companion before his accident.

'When Lad died at the age of fourteen I had never felt so devastated in my life — it was like losing a childhood friend,' Kris says in a way which shows that he still mourns the loss. 'People might think it's silly to have been so upset over an animal but in this case it was special. Lad was closer to me than Czar can be because he could remember how, before my accident, I used to romp with him, which of course is something that I can never do with Czar.

'When I was in Stoke Mandeville they once brought Lad to see me. It's a lovely hospital with spacious grounds and a lot of greenery so it was no problem to meet the dog outside. I hadn't seen him for a long time when they brought him to see me. I called to him, and he ran over to me and there was great joy between the two of us.

'While I had been away he had got lost — you can image how upsetting that was — and then he was found at the Battersea Dogs' Home. Somehow he had caught a disease which nearly killed him. The vet actually wanted to put him down, but my Mum knew what he meant to me and wouldn't let him, and luckily she managed to nurse him through.

'When he was better he was brought to see me, and I vividly remember how cracked the skin of his nose was — funny the little things that come back to you. The house my parents owned at the time had sitting tenants on the ground floor, and they left the door open . . .

'Speaking of that, the Southwark Council was very good because when I came out of hospital they told them that I had to be on the ground floor, and that they would have to move, and they found them another place. But in the end that house proved to be too difficult — there was no bathroom downstairs, and it was not suitable for a wheelchair.

'So the council decided to fix up this place for me. It's ideal, they made the doorways wide enough for a wheelchair, and all the electric sockets are at the right level — very important when you can't bend down to the floor. I got all the equipment I need such as a hoist, intercom systems so that if I am ever in trouble I can have word with someone upstairs, and an alarm outside. So they did a very good job for me providing that kind of thing. But it is thanks to the MFPA that I got the extras which make the difference between a bearable life and a fulfilling life.

Today Kris continues to work hard at his art, producing a finished painting on average of once a fortnight though he does not work with the same desperation as he did when he was a student anxious to get full membership of the association. He found that once he became a full member his painting became easier and actually improved, perhaps because the membership gave him a new-found confidence in his work.

He works in oils using very short handled brushes which, while they give him greater control of the paint, do have the disadvantage of putting a strain on his eyesight through working with his face so close to the canvas.

'I like to work with very thin paints because I find that I can work the paint a lot better,' he explains. 'I like very controlled, tight paintings. Every speck of paint I put down I put there deliberately — not because the brush happened to hit there.

'I put my paintings straight on to the canvas after drawing the outlines in paint — not pencil — and in my mind I know exactly what I want to do. Sometimes I do a paint sketch of what I'm going to do so that I know what's going to go where, and then do the painting straight off on the bare canvas.'

Kris' paintings which are reproduced are usually portraits or landscapes. Much of his inspiration for the latter comes from journeys made into the countryside in his specially equipped van, his favourite spot being Devil's Dyke in Sussex. Finding it difficult to work out of doors, he gets photographs taken of scenes which are potential paintings but even these do present problems.

'If I am going somewhere interesting my brother takes my camera along but the trouble is that when people take photographs for you they never see the scene exactly as you do,' he says. 'There is one point at Devil's Dyke where the trees arch over the road so that it looks like a tunnel of foliage. I would have loved to have painted this and I gave directions how I wanted it photographed. I could see it perfectly in my mind's eye as though I was looking through the viewfinder, yet when I got the prints it seemed a completely different picture to me.'

Apart from the paintings which Kris has published, he paints others which

116

are mainly for himself — surreal paintings which indicate the inner, imaginative world which he has built up to replace parts of the outer world which he has lost. The possibilities of surrealism are endless, he declares. And when he is doing such a painting he has the feeling of being able to create anything he likes on the canvas — he is in charge in a way that his disability prevents him from being in other aspects of life, he creates his own worlds with oil paint.

These surreal paintings have a lot in common with the work of those elite artists of the book jacket world who specialize in sophisticated science fiction themes. One of Kris' recent surreal paintings shows the pyramids at the bottom of the picture while above them a woman is tumbling down from heaven, a woman who has wings where her arms would normally be. Another picture, particularly striking because of its evocative use of sunset light, shows a blonde woman in evening dress on a barren outcrop of rock leaning forward to help a cat on the skeletal branch of a dead tree. Who the woman is, why she is in evening dress in this wilderness, and the significance of the cat Kris does not explain — it was a picture which grew in his imagination and which he painted from his inner vision with the same surety with which he paints a landscape from a photograph.

One only has to talk to Kris for a while to get an inkling of how active his imagination has become since he has been confined to a wheelchair.

'I like to think there is some magic in the world,' he says. 'I'd like to think that unicorns once existed, and amazing heroes like Hercules and Ulysses. — In fact, I am sure that Homer's story about the Trojan War is true — after all the ruins of Troy were discovered by working out its position from clues given in the Iliad. And it's the same with religion, I *prefer* to believe. No one can say definitely whether there is a God or life after death, but those who believe do have the consolation and uplift of their faith through life and if they are wrong and there is nothing it does not matter because they will never know . . .'

When the conversation comes round to such matters the question of Kris' attitude to his disability arises.

'I guess if I was OK I'd probably be married,' he says. 'But then a lot of people who are married regret it, so it's hard to say.

'What I do regret is not being able to play sport, especially as a lot of my friends who I went to school with still take part in it. For me rugby was not just a game, it was a way of life at the Christopher Wren School. The head boy was always a rugby player and this was nearly always the case with prefects. You got privileges if you were good at rugby and you got on better with the teachers. Although a London comprehensive, it was rugby mad, and I loved it. Now it's a mixed school and has some horrendous new name which I find upsetting when I look back on it . . .

'I find it's best not to dwell about the past — if you thought about it to much you'd go crazy. I try just to concentrate on the things that I am good at today and keep them to the forefront. I can't play rugby anymore but I play a lot of chess — sometimes by telephone with Charles Fowler. And I can give my computer a good game.

'But I must admit there have been times when I thought God had been unfair, but then how can one expect life to be perfect?

'Now I think I am unlucky compared with a lot of people, and very lucky compared with a lot of others. People often say it but it is true, there is always someone worse off than you. And I think of this when I see famine pictures from Ethiopia, and when I've encountered dossers down the road and have seen drug addicts whose minds are completely gone, I wonder what the hell I'm complaining about.

'Compared with such people I'm doing all right. My family has been a tremendous help, in fact they have kept me sane and helped me come to terms with my disability. And I have the support of very good district nurses who come in the morning to help my parents get me up and at night to help me go to bed.

'In the five years before I got in touch with the MFPA I spent most of my time in the house in front of the television set, the idea of travel and mobility seeming beyond me. In those days I had a lot of things listed that I dearly wanted to do, but when I look at the list now it gets smaller and smaller. Life has become so much fuller and painting has given me a reason for living.'

Kris' latest interest is astronomy. During the summer nights when he can sit out in the garden without feeling cold he spends hours scanning the night sky with a special telescope which he can operate himself.

'When you look into the infinity of space it certainly gets things into perspective,' Kris says, and with a hint of his magical imagination adds, 'And with so many hundreds of galaxies in the universe I like to think that everyone has their own particular star.'

'There's Only One Way
To Go . . .'

HEATHER STRUDWICK

WHEN at the age of 23, Heather Strudwick was admitted to hospital with an undiagnosed complaint, she had no inkling that, apart from the physical pain she was about to suffer, it was a prelude to a series of almost unbearable losses including her husband, baby son and home. Until that fateful day in 1957 she had been a happy, carefree young woman with a will of her own which she says she inherited from her father making her a 'chip off the old block'. As things were to turn out it was very fortunate that she was such a chip.

Heather's father was a lance corporal stationed in Gibraltar when she was born in 1933 and her childhood was spent in various countries to which he was posted. Her happiest memories are of Egypt and today her face lightens as she describes how she and her sister would go horse riding in the cool of the early morning. When she grew up she trained to become an orthopaedic nurse in Oxford.

It was during this time that she fell in love with her future husband, and when he had completed his national service and joined the police force, they married and set up home in Colchester. Here their son Paul was born, and later Heather took a job as an industrial nurse at a factory in the town, and it seemed that everything was right with the world.

Heather was riding her bicycle to work one day in 1957 when she felt an ache in her back. At first she did nothing about it, explaining later that when you have a home to manage as well as a job you cannot go running to the doctor with every little pain that you get. But later, when she found difficulty in breathing she did seek medical advice and was sent to the local hospital.

'At that point I just had backache followed by the inability to breathe,' she recalls. 'Because my diaphragm became paralysed I started breathing rather fast and shallow, and the result of that was to over-ventilate so that I got stiff hands and stiff feet — which is a typical symptom of hysteria. When I arrived in hospital I was so ticked off for breathing like that and I think they thought they were dealing with a hysterical young woman who had had a row with her husband or something like that. So I had a very dodgy twenty-four hours until I was moved to another ward where I had a lumbar puncture. Then my breathing went completely so I was put into an iron lung.'

Now there could be no doubt — Heather had become a victim of poliomyelitis.

'I don't blame them for not diagnosing it at once,' she says of that traumatic period. 'It was not easy because there was nothing for them to go on. Because there had not been any other cases of polio in the district it was the last thing they were looking for, and I did not have the usual outward symptoms of a headache, cold and sore throat.'

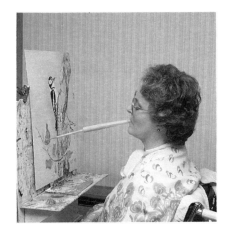

Heather was transferred to the Rush Green Hospital in Romford which, at the time, was the respiratory centre for Essex. Here she spent all her time in the iron lung, in great pain and trying to cope with the knowledge that she was completely paralysed. This was coupled with the natural concern she felt over her husband and her twenty-month-old son Paul.

Six weeks passed before she was allowed to see him, and then he was stood outside a window instead of being brought into the ward where there was a risk of infection. It seemed that he was unable to recognize his mother — only her head protruded from the coffin-like tank which was keeping her alive — and this brought home to her as much as anything the hopelessnes of her situation. It was a relief when it was agreed that her sister-in-law Sheila would take care of the child for the time being, but worry over her husband increased. At first he visited her like any anxious husband would, then the intervals between visits lengthened and after having promised to see her, he would not turn up at all, which left Heather crying after the ward lights had been switched off. To add to her mental turmoil it was discovered that she was pregnant and was given the choice of whether or not she should be operated on. It was an agonizing dilemma to face, especially during the hours of darkness when she felt alone with the sound of the lung's bellows as an endless obligato to her thoughts, but in the end she agreed to the operation. When it was all over she was told that the baby was dead.

The hospital authorities became anxious over the effect the infrequency of her husband's visits was having upon their patient and they got in touch with the police station he was attached to, saying that he must be given leave to visit his wife who was so ill. A surprised voice at the other end of the line replied that not only had he been granted special leave but he had been given money to cover travelling expenses.

'He was using it to take his lady friend out,' Heather explains. 'The truth was that he had found someone else. This shock was followed by another. My sister-in-law announced that if she was to continue looking after my son she wanted to adopt him. She wrote: "We don't want to love Paul and then lose him, but if you will agree to us legally adopting him then you will make us all happy. If not, then perhaps you could make an arrangmeent for someone else to look after him."

'Until then I hadn't realized that I was not going to get any better — that it would be impossible for me to do anything for Paul and that I had to lose him. But I found that when you hit rock bottom there's only one way to go — and that's up. I also had an experience which did me a lot of good. There was a young cadet nurse on the ward — a very nice and very sensitive girl — who used to do a lot for me personally as well as feed me and so on. On this particular day the food trolley was wheeled into the ward, and the nurses stood round it waiting for the meals each had to feed a patient. And sister said to this youngster, "Here's Heather's dinner, nurse, if you will feed her."

'They did not realize that I could hear them, and I heard my special nurse say to sister, "Must I?"

'Sister was surprised because she thought that we got on very well, and she said, "Yes nurse. Why, what's wrong?"

'"Oh," she replied, "She's always crying."

'I was absolutely devastated when I heard this. I thought about it, and I decided she was absolutely right — she was so kind and so nice that I was burdening her with all my problems and at eighteen she could not take it, and shouldn't have had to take it anyway.

'It was a hard lesson but a good one, and when I got it sorted out in my head I realized that, if I had to be fed and looked after for the rest of my life, I had to make the people who helped me laugh and not cry. So that was the turning point.'

Heather's husand wanted a divorce and, as it was more difficult in those days, she said she would agree if he gave his consent to Paul's adoption. 'By then I knew that I could not look after him, and it was his welfare that was the most important, that mattered most,' Heather says. 'He had to have security, and as my sister-in-law wanted to adopt him I felt that she must love him, so she eventually adopted him and then I divorced my husband.'

Heather was to remain in the hospital at Romford for five years, the first two of which she spent in an iron lung. The first thing that she had to learn was a method of getting air into lungs known as 'frog breathing' in which the patient uses the tongue as a pump instead of the paralysed diaphraghm.

'It took me quite a while to master,' Heather recalls, 'but as I learned the technique it meant that I was able to stay outside the lung for longer and longer periods during which I was able to sit in a wheelchair although I only had a limited movement in my neck. The trouble was that it was quite exhausting work which made my heart beat faster which in turn made me out of breath.

'In those days portable respirators had not been perfected and it was only through frog breathing that I could enjoy any freedom from the tank. Today, with portable respirators, which work like a lung regularly inflated and deflated, I only frog breathe for short periods such as when I am disconnected from the respirator which is fitted to my wheelchair, to go to the bedroom where I sleep in a conventional iron lung. And it is comforting to know that should there be a power failure I can keep going under my own steam until my standby generator is started up.'

But during those years spent in Romford's Rush Green Hospital the idea of living an independent life in the outside world seemed an impossible dream, and the most Heather could hope for was a brief wheelchair outing. Because her parents were separated they had no home to offer her though they visited her frequently, and one day her father arrived with the news that he had had his car specially adapted to take her out. To Heather's delight her doctors decided that she could go out with him for a period of an hour — and after having felt so confined for so long what a magical hour it was.

'I was excited like a child,' Heather remembers enthusiastically. 'It was a beautiful April day but until we reached the countryside I found the noise of the traffic frightening. Then we were driving along peaceful lanes and the world seemed all colour!'

As the car cruised through the Essex lanes Heather realized that if she could learn to frog breathe for up to eight hours her horizons would be limitless. She persevered and in August, 1959, with the help of two nursing sisters who took along a portable respirator to reassure her, she flew for a week's holiday to Belgium where he father, now a colonel, was stationed. Apart from the much-needed break from hospital routine, the effect of the trip was to give her the impetus to make the best of her situation no matter how difficult it might be.

In 1960 it was decided that Heather should go for a special course of physiotheraphy at the Nuffield Orthopaedic Centre at Oxford — the same hospital where she had done her nursing training. She found that the sister she had been under was still there, and she was overwhelmed with kindness by her ex-colleagues. Doctors at the Nuffield came to the conclusion that while frog breathing allowed Heather to come out of her iron lung, it did not allow her to do or attempt any other activity. The result was that she was fitted with a newly developed Thompston Pneumabelt portable respirator which operates like an inflatable corset which by steady inflation and deflation, forces air in and out of the patient's lungs.

Freed from having to consciously breathe all the time, Heather's first step was to learn to type by means of a stick held in her mouth which which she jabbed at the keys. At times she was almost in despair because her aim was erratic and it seemed that what she typed appeared like a secret code as more letters appeared by mistake than intention.

When Heather finally became proficient with a friend in the hospital and, with a wry sense of humour, it was named *Puffin.* Twenty copies of the first edition were distributed, and it was so successful that the circulation climbed to the thousand mark and its income was used for the purchase of a private ambulance for the other respiratory patients in Ward 11a of the hospital.

Heather was on her way again.

In 1963, when she had been in hospital at Romford for five years, Heather asked if it would be possible for her to be transferred to the Mylands Hospital in Colchester because she felt that her roots were in that town, having spent the latter part of her schooling there after her father had been stationed there. Her faithful Colchester friends were still making the journey to visit her and she wanted to be back amongst them.

It was after this move that Heather made her first attempt at painting.

'Strangely, I never enjoyed art at school,' Heather says. 'And it would never have occurred to me to try it in hospital — especially being so paralysed — if I had not been nagged by a friend of mine who thought I ought to be doing something. He gave me a copy of the book *God's Second Door* about mouth

and foot painters, and after reading it I thought "Good heavens, no way could I paint like that!" But to please my friend I did try — holding a brush in my mouth — and found that I enjoyed it! Of course my first efforts were what you would expect, the paint seemed to run everywhere and my brush strokes wobbled all over the place. But I kept trying, and I think it appealed to me so much because it was the only thing I could start and finish myself — something that I could do my way.'

In the hope of improving her technique Heather did go to night school from hospital for a short time but she recalls that it was rather a disaster because everyone became so interested in watching the way she worked that she did not get taught anything. And she found that the basic techniques used by able-bodied painters, such as stretching out one's arm with a pencil held to measure the perspective, were obviously impossible for her.

'I had to go it alone and develop my own techniques,' Heather explains. 'Later on I was greatly helped by a local artist named Bill Burton. He is a very talented man and he did more for me because he told me about colours, and he would loan me his own pictures to copy and then explain exactly how he got various effects. But I really learned by trial and error . . . and just struggling on. Mind you, it was no chore because I loved doing it.

'Had I not got polio I probably never would have painted so that is something good which came out of it. It has meant so much, apart from the fact that it enabled me to become financially independent later on . . .'

In 1964, encouraged by the fact that people were actually asking for her paintings, Heather got in touch with the Mouth and Foot Painting Artists Association which she had learned about through the book *God's Second Door*. Her paintings were evaluated and she was given a scholarship to enable her to continue with her efforts to become a proficient artist.

The next year there was a new face among the people who helped Heather in hospital. It was a man named Ron Strudwick who had taken on a job as hospital porter so that, having been widowed, he could live in Colchester with his daughter.

'We met in mid-air,' Heather recalls with a warmth which still mirrors the happiness of those days. 'He used to lift me out of bed into my wheelchair. Soon he began to look in and say hello when he was passing. And by lunchtime he would bring his sandwiches and sit beside me when I was painting outside in my wheelchair. He would squeeze out fresh paint or adjust the canvas on my easel and chat to me in a most entertaining way. I soon realized that he had an intuitive understanding, but one day I felt it necessary that I should ask him why he spent so much time with me. *Was it out of pity?* That was something I had to know.'

Ron Strudwick replied that it had not occurred to him — he just enjoyed her company.

'Then he asked me to go out — just as if I were a normal person,' says Heather. 'It was rather nice, and he took me to Felixstowe in his car for the afternoon.

'As we became increasingly fond of each other I decided that his friendship must either progress or be knocked rather smartly on the head, so we consulted the doctor and he told Ron that I might live for two days or twenty years. Then he wished us the best of luck.'

The same year Heather had a chance to fulfill a long standing ambition, but it was a challenge which required every scrap of courage that she could muster. She was offered the opportunity of visiting her sister Patricia who lived in Ann Arbor in Michigan, USA. Despite the difficulties, and the physical strain she knew it would entail, she accepted enthusiastically and her father made arrangements for her to sail on the old *Queen Elizabeth*.

'I had to take a rocking bed and a portable respirator with me, but on board I was treated like royalty,' Heather says. 'Cunard even provided a special nurse for me at no extra charge, and I had two stewards allocated to help me every day. They would come down to the cabin as soon as I was dressed, and they would take me all over the ship.

'My travelling companion was an old lady of seventy-three — she was the only person I could find who could pay her own fare because, as I was still living in the hospital then and had not started painting professionally, I had no money. Of course she could not lift me, but she was able to get help from other people.'

Heather's adventures on her own began when the liner docked in New York. A famous American organization, The March of Dimes, had booked a hotel room for her and installed a rocking bed in it, a rocking bed being pivoted in the middle so that an electric motor operates it like a see-saw to cause the patient's diaphragm to inflate and deflate the lungs with the up-and-down motion. Heather's problem was to get herself and her elderly companion to the hotel.

A Yellow Cab was ordered and when it arrived at the quayside Heather was bundled into the front seat before the driver realized she was disabled. But, in the tradition of New York cabbies, he was unperturbed when he learned that his fare was paralysed from the neck down, and when their destination was reached he insisted on carrying her to her room.

Heather spent the night on the rocking bed — it is obviously impossible to frog breathe when one is asleep — and the next day she was taken to the airport where The March of Dimes had arranged for her to travel on a military ambulance aircraft. When she was carried aboard on a stretcher she found that there were two doctors and five nurses to care for her. And, as she remarked afterwards, she never had her blood pressure taken so many times as on that flight to Michigan.

Heather felt that she could not be more delighted than when she was reunited with her sister who, being a poet and artist in her own right, was very sympathetic and encouraging over her efforts to become a professional painter, but there was one unexpected happening in store which made her cup of happiness brim over. On the fourth day of her stay someone walked into her sister's home and she looked up to see Ron Strudwick whose visit had been arranged by Patricia as a surprise gift.

It did not take Ron long to suggest that they should get married right away. In one way Heather was delighted with the idea — it would be lovely to have her sister at the wedding, but it would be terribly disappointing for her parents, and her friends who had been so faithful over the last eight difficult years, not to be at the ceremony. And then a solution struck them — why not get married twice? No one in England need know about the Michigan wedding until much later, and this way no one would be disappointed.

'The result was that four days later we were secretly married by a Justice of the Peace,' says Heather. 'It took place in a garden beneath an apple tree pink with blossom, and it could not have been more romantic — until the official turned round and gave us the advantage of his back view, and we saw that he was wearing an open necked shirt, shorts and sandals. He had thrown his gown over these casual clothes and, with his bare legs, he looked quite naked from the back.

'Ron and I had three glorious weeks together before he had to fly back to England, and during this period my sister instructed him in looking after me.'

When the time came for Heather to leave Ann Arbor she was confronted by an unexpected problem. So many wounded soldiers were being brought back from Vietnam that there was no room for her in a military aircraft, and no commercial airline would accept her with her breathing problems. Somehow she had to get to New York to catch the *Queen Elizabeth*, and in the end it was decided to smuggle her on to an ordinary passenger aircraft.

Her ticket was bought and somehow, while she did her frog breathing furiously, friends half-carried her aboard and in the crush the cabin staff did not notice that there was anything unusual about her. It was only when the aircraft had landed at New York and all the other passengers had disembarked that the air hostesses approached the solitary figure who remained seated.

'Is there anything wrong? — you are supposed to get out here,' said one.

'There's nothing wrong but I need someone to carry me off,' Heather answered.

In the autumn of that year Heather and Ron had their second wedding

with family members and friends present, and a few months later they were able to move into a bungalow of their own. To have a home of her own again after ten years of hospitalization was something which had been beyond Heather's wildest dream, but there she was sharing it with a man she loved and who was devoted to her.

Looking back to this idyllic time, Heather says, 'After the way my first marriage had ended I could hardly believe how fortunate I was to experience real love after being paralysed for so long. Ron was a very special person, completely selfless and though he was older than me it made no more difference to our relationship than my disability. We just lived for each other and used to joke that we were two old fogies, but in fact we were so happy that we didn't need anything else. I used to tell him, "Night is such a waste of time because we're both unconscious".'

During this time Heather continued working at her painting, producing pictures whose hallmark was clear, bright colours, a technique which may have been subconsciously inspired by the day when Heather was able to leave the hospital for the first time and 'the world seemed all colour'. She had begun with watercolours but like other disabled artists did not find them satisfactory. Acrylics were tried next but these dried too quickly for her purpose, and it was only with oils that she found the perfect medium. It was her ambition to reach a standard which would give her full membership of the Mouth and Foot Painters Association.

The world which Heather and Ron built up over the next five years came to an end when he was taken ill and soon afterwards died in hospital, leaving Heather not only to cope with her overwhelming grief but the added problem of being once more a disabled person on her own. The local authorities wanted her to go back to hospital but the one thing that she clung to through the first shattering fortnight was the determination to remain in the home which she and Ron had built up together.

Heather's father came to stay with her and her doctor agreed to her remaining in her bungalow for a trial period of six months. Now the problem was to find people who would look after her as at that time the authorities would not pay for resident help. A group of fourteen elderly lady volunteers was organized, working on a system which meant that there was a rota of six to come in each day. It turned out to be an unsatisfactory arrangement because each new arrival wanted to chat and in effect be entertained which meant that Heather became exhausted through being a day-long hostess. She had not time for painting or following events in the outside world through television, and in one of the saddest remarks it is possible to make she said, 'I was not allowed to have the time to grieve.'

But when the six-month period was up Heather was still adamant that she did not want to be institutionalized again. For a while an old age pensioner looked after her, until a combination of arthritis and diabetes made it impossible for her to continue.

At this time it was decided that Heather needed a hip operation, and for this she was taken to St Thomas' Hospital in London. This hospital had assumed responsbility for the respiratory cases of the whole country because, being few in number and gradually diminishing, it was considered best to centralise the work. At the time the hospital was running a project to discover if it was cost effective for people with such a disability to be maintained in their own homes rather than remain in hospital. Thanks to the hip operation bringing Heather to their notice, those in charge of the project allowed her to join it which meant from then on she would have paid residential help.

It looked at though her independence was assured but Heather was to find that it opened the door to further problems — problems which highlighted one of the major worries of the disabled. This was the question of being able to get the right helpers. At first girls were employed but Heather was conscious that the work was a burden for them with only one day off a week and unable to go out in the evenings — at the age of eighteen Heather believed that they should be able to have a complete break from looking after her.

Advertisements were placed for more mature help, and Heather had to cope with some applicants who were unsuitable, to put it mildly. One turned out to be an alcoholic who, while Heather was having a check-up, went on a drinking spree and then vanished, leaving her charge to return to a wrecked home.

In the spring of 1974 it seemed that the right person had come along at last. A woman, Lisa, got in touch with Heather through an advertisement she had inserted in *The Lady* for a helper.

At the interview on a Friday afternoon she seemed to be exatly the right sort of person to be Heather's housekeeper, being in her early forties and explaining that she had just left a family where she had been helping to look after the wife who had just died. Because she was no longer needed there, she told Heather it would be possible for her to move in the next day . . .

'That would be fantastic,' a relieved Heather told her.

The new housekeeper arrived on Saturday morning and Heather felt they were going to get along fine, and the only thing that seemed a little odd occurred in the late afternoon when Lisa said, 'Do you mind if I put my suitcase in the garden shed?'

'It'll get damp out there,' Heather replied. 'It would be better if you stored it in the bungalow loft.'

'I'd rather keep it in the shed.'

'All right,' said Heather with a mental shrug. She remembers that the next day was a very pleasant one with her new companion, but on the Monday morning she woke at six o'clock in the iron lung and saw that the sliding doors to Lisa's room were partly open, and that beyond them the bed was made. Next she heard a movement in the living room and called out to ask Lisa if she was all right.

The housekeeper came into Heather's room and explained that she had suffered with cramp in her legs all night long.

'Do you mind if I go for a long walk?' she asked. 'Excercise always puts it right.'

Heather felt that if this would help she had to agree. Lisa made her a cup of tea and, putting on her coat, said, 'I'll take the dog for a walk if you like.'

The dog was in fact Sacha, a black poodle bitch, who had been given to her by her father soon after her husband's death, and because of her amusing ways and deeply affectionate nature had become Heather's dearest companion.

'Sacha would like that,' said Heather, and off went Lisa with the little dog trotting after her on her lead.

A little while later Heather's home help arrived and assisted her to get up but by eleven o'clock the housekeeper had not returned and she began to feel anxious.

'You ought to ring somebody up,' advised the home help, but there was no one to whom Heather could turn. Then the home help said, 'I wonder if she has enough money on her to come back by bus. I'll go and see if she has taken her handbag with her.'

A moment later she returned from Lisa's room with the news that not only was there no handbag but her clothes were gone. Heather's heart seemed to turn over when the home help went out to the garden shed and found that the suitcase was missing as well.

'I rang the police but they said she could not be classed as a missing person until she had been gone for thirty-six hours,' Heather recalls. 'And when I protested that she had taken my dog they could not have cared less. Then, by the evening, I discovered that she had taken all my money, so that became theft. I rang the police again, and they came round here very quickly. The inspector in charge of the case was really sweet — he could see how upset I was — and I think he thought that the next time it could be a child that she might take. Apparently Lisa had been in and out of prison for the past twenty years for going into people's houses as a housekeeper and making off with their belongings.

'In my case she had already put her loot in the suitcase which she took out of the shed when she went off with Sacha to the bus-stop where she

131

took a bus to the railway station, and vanished.'

The next Heather heard of her erstwhile housekeeper was when the police announced that she had been arrested in an old people's home in Scotland where she was doing her usual routine. She admitted that she had taken a train from Colchester on which she found that people spoke to her about Sacha, as dog-lovers will do, and she was afraid that she might be traced through the poodle. When the train reached Cambridge she pushed the little dog out of the carriage.

Everyone realized how important Sacha was to Heather. Her home help and her husband offered a £100 reward, the story of the lost pet was told on Anglia Television, and the police began an intensive search in the Cambridge area. This involved checking all the dog pound records for the district and one entry relating to a lost black poodle bitch, dated a week after she had been taken from Heather, sent a police officer hurrying to a pound where he learned she had been sold a week after she had been taken in. The new owner was contacted and after a three-week separation a woe-begone Sacha was returned to her mistress. She looked half-starved and dirty, with a wound on one hip, and her eyes were so cloudy that for a sickening moment Heather feared that her pet had gone blind. But Sacha recognized her and with a whimper of contentment settled on her lap and fell into a deep sleep.

The question of helpers is no longer a problem as they are provided by the hospital and the local authority after the Chronically Sick and Disabled Persons Act had been invoked on Heather's behalf. She now has two young women to help her, each of whom stays continuously at her bungalow for three-and-a-half days each week. This is an ideal solution for all concerned as it allows the helpers to have enough time for themselves in a flat provided for them close to Heather's bungalow.

It seemed the tide had turned in Heather's favour at last, and this has been added to by her relationship with Paul, her son who she agreed to have adopted so long ago.

'My sister-in-law Sheila has been wonderful over Paul,' Heather declares. 'She has shared him with me, and when he was at school she used to ring me up to read out his reports and things like that. It has been a delicate situation but I am happy to say we never fell out — not once.'

'Now Paul is grown up and has his own central heating business, and comes to visit me with his wife and two grandchildren Martin and Sharon. They send me a card on Mother's Day which means a great deal to me. I think he finds the situation much easier to handle now that he has got his own home and family, because while he was living with Sheila his loyalty was to her first while his relationship with me was not so close.

'The first thing that happened regarding the situation was when he was sixteen. One afternoon I had my wheelchair out in the garden, having a cup of tea with some friends, when he dropped in with a friend of his to show off his new motorbike. Of course I had to introduce him, and I did so as my son. I saw his friend give him a very puzzled look, so the next time he came I had to talk to him about it. I said, "Look, I do love you to come, but if you come when I have people I have to introduce you as somebody, and you *are* my son.' He understood that, and I added that it was up to him to explain the situation to his friends.'

Heather Strudwick's proudest day came in March, 1982, when she was made a full member of the Mouth and Foot Painters Association. This meant that, apart from having made the grade as a professional artist, she would enjoy financial independence. And what a joyous moment it was when she wrote to the Social Security authorities to inform them that after receiving assistance for over twenty years she no longer required it because she was now able to support herself.

'It was the best letter I have ever written in my life, thanks to the MFPA,' she says. 'And it is through them that I have been able to buy a little cottage, very close to my home, for my mother to live in. It is wonderful when you have been on the receiving end of so much kindness, to be able to do something for someone else.'

Today Heather continues to paint, working at least three afternoons a week for three hours at a time.

'My style of painting has only changed from earlier on in that I can now tackle more difficult subjects,' she says. 'I love painting birds and animals. They are really my first love and my style goes with whatever turns me on. When I start painting I know roughly the colours I shall need, and a helper puts them out in blobs so that I can mix them myself, the difficult part is keeping the colours the same because I paint in bits and occasionally paint upside down because I cannot reach across the whole canvas.

'It takes me three weeks to a month to complete a picture, depending on how quickly it dries, as you can't paint on top of wet paint so usually I have three on the go at once.

'When I was able to get my own vehicle to go out in I tried sketching and painting in the country but I found that this was impossible so I use reference books, and I find the video extremely useful — if there is a scene I like I can record it and then put it on hold which is ideal for backgrounds.

'I painted a lot in hospital — a great advantage was that I did not have to think about food or shopping which, of course, I have to now. And the painting was a great outlet for me, it is a great thing to be able to do it.'

Thanks to her hard won independence, Heather is able to take a great delight out of things which the able-bodied take for granted.

'I love to go on a big shopping spree at least once a month and buy all the heavy stuff — giant big packets of washing powder and things like that,' she says with relish. 'To me the shops are still like Aladdin's caves, and I love pottering around them. I have to have a list otherwise I get sidetracked and spend too much money and — like a typical woman — I window shop a great deal. And the other thing I love to do is to go out into the country and just sit in my wheelchair, listening to the trees.'

Heather says that in her dreams she is not disabled except when she cannot breathe properly and then she dreams that someone has disconnected her iron lung from its power supply.

'Otherwise my dreams are all active and in colour,' she says. 'They are very pleasurable. I have the best of both worlds . . . active by night and waited on hand, foot and finger during the day!

'When I look back on my life I think I am awfully lucky because I have done everything — I *do* know what it's like to swim, to run, to dance and to ride. When I see someone riding on television — eventing or whatever — I can almost smell the horse. I know what the leather smells like when it's damp.

'And I had a normal marriage and a baby until I got polio, and afterwards I was lucky to have another very special marriage. People who are born disabled, or disabled very young, have not had the chances that I had. Some say that by being disabled later on you have more to miss, but I don't see it that way. I like to feel that I know what it's like — and then I think I've got to shut the door on regrets and just carry on.'